MARKETING YOUR SERVICE BUSINESS

IAN RUSKIN-BROWN

9

Viva Books Private Limited
New Delhi • Mumbai • Chennai • Kolkata • Bangalore • Hyderabad

First Indian Edition 2007

VIVA BOOKS PRIVATE LIMITED

- 4737/23 Ansari Road, Daryaganj, New Delhi 110 002
  E-mail: vivadelhi@vivagroupindia.net, Tel. 42242200
- Plot No. 76, Service Industries, Shirvane, Sector 1, Nerul, Navi Mumbai 400 706
  E-mail: vivamumbai@vivagroupindia.net, Tel. 27721273, 27721274
- Jamals Fazal Chambers, 26 Greams Road, Chennai 600 006
  E-mail: vivachennai@vivagroupindia.net, Tel. 28290304, 28294241
- B-103, Jindal Towers, 21/1A/3 Darga Road, Kolkata 700 017
  E-mail: vivakolkata@vivagroupindia.net, Tel. 22836381, 22816713
- 7, Sovereign Park Apartments, 56-58, K. R. Road, Basavanagudi, Bangalore 560 004
  E-mail: vivabangalore@vivagroupindia.net, Tel. 26607409, 26607410
- 101-102 Mughal Marc Apartments, 3-4-637 to 641, Narayanguda, Hyderabad 500 029
  E-mail: vivahyderabad@vivagroupindia.net, Tel. 27564481, 27564482

Published by arrangement with

Thorogood Publishers Limited
10-12 Rivington Street
London EC2A 3DU,
UK

ISBN 81-309-0342-3

Published by Vinod Vasishtha for Viva Books Private Limited, 4737/23 Ansari Road, Daryaganj, New Delhi 110 002.

Printed by Sanat Printers, Kundli - 131028.

The author

For the last 26 years Ian Ruskin-Brown, the author, has been the owner/ entrepreneur of several service businesses. These have included:

- Property management and the provision of student accommodation
- An international market research company, and
- A consultancy and international training business.

Ian ran a market research company – Marketing Decisions International Ltd – from 1980 to 1994. The company was a full member of the Market Research Society. It was through these businesses that Ian conducted many market research and consultancy projects for firms in the service sector: from government organizations (BBC, HM Customs & Excise) to the Law Society, several national and international airlines, banks and building societies.

Ian was course director at the Chartered Institute of Marketing for courses on marketing in the service sector (1984-1998). These courses ran around 12 times per year, peaking to 16 per annum from 1992 to 1995.

Additionally, Ian designed, wrote and piloted in-company training courses on marketing and selling consultancy services for a number of blue chip companies including:

- The IBM Marketing University
- ICL Training, and
- Kodak Health Imaging.

He currently runs the *Marketing Your Services* course for Management Center Europe (part of the American Marketing Association). These are scheduled to run as open courses three times per annum. He also runs client specific courses in the USA and South East Asia.

Ian Ruskin-Brown can be contacted at ian@ruskin-brownassociates.com and www.ruskin-brownassociates.com

Contents

Introduction

As in his previous book, *Mastering Marketing*, the author writes here primarily for the practicing business manager or entrepreneur whose business is:

1. In the service sector (from hotels, through grooming, and via travel and tourism, design and consultancy, through to financial services, medical health care and professional advice), or
2. Uses services and/or 'service products' (e.g. training, design, stock management, upgrades, warranties) to gain a Competitive Differential Advantage (CDA) by adding value for its customers.

For this target group, this latest book provides a practical and intensive grounding in the special techniques for marketing when the 'product' is either fully or partly a service.

Understanding how to employ and market services is *the* critical business issue of today's world for both the manufacturing and service sectors. In the developed world, the service sector continues to grow apace, while the manufacturing sector is static or in decline.

Services are traditionally the engines of an economy's recovery, and interestingly 'new starts' in this sector are more likely to survive than those starting out in the 'goods' sectors. Ron Zemke[1] found that of the new start-ups in the service sector, some 80% survived the first two years – nearly twice the survival rate of those producing goods.

In the developed and developing world, economic growth is a result of business-related forces plus the changes taking place in their societies.

In business-to-business (B2B) markets, services are not confined to the service sector – if, in reality, they ever were. They are widely used by many firms in the 'goods' sector to build value for the customer and create the firm's CDA. For example:

- IBM, never noted for its 'competitive prices,' depends critically on 'customer service' to keep its >50% share of the market in the USA.
- The USA Office of Trade has shown that some 75% of the value added in their various manufacturing sectors comes via 'services'.

There are reasons for this. Providing customers with good services:

- can be an effective way of avoiding devastating price competition and,
- are the fastest, most efficient and efficacious ways of building customer relationships.

An important reason for the great interest in the service sector is that it accounts for c. 70% of Gross Domestic Product (GDP) in the developed world. This, however, may be a huge distortion of the truth in favor of 'goods.' The accounting systems of most governments are still based on their 'old economies' which were traditionally dominated by, for example, farming, extraction, manufacturing (i.e. goods).

Services don't replace manufacturing, they complement and facilitate. However, most services used in the manufacturing sectors are hidden and not exploited for their CDA potential as well as they could be. These services include billing, claims handling, deliveries and financial services etc., etc.

With the resurgence of the low cost of production economics such as India and China, there is pressure to break away from the use of sheer technical innovation for future CDAs. That route is slow, expensive, not guaranteed to work commercially and can be relatively easy to copy or 'work around'.

Firms now have to offer a compendium of services extra to the aforementioned, such as technical back-up, repair and maintenance, inventory management, training and financial facilitation[2].

Societal changes taking place globally outweigh the consumers' traditional under-valuation of services in favor of goods (i.e. the tangibles). In the developed world there is strong growth in demand from consumer markets[3] as priorities change from 'survival' to 'experiential' services, for example, restaurants, tourism, entertainment, sports and health. That is why understanding how to employ and market services is today's critical issue for both manufacturing and the service sectors. Most management and marketing theory, however, is based on experience and/or research in the 'goods' sector (mostly FMCGs) and too often in the B2C markets.

Whilst this book is based on sound principles established by research and experience and is academically sound, it is written primarily for the practitioner, not the academic. It does, however, assume some basic knowledge of marketing[4] so that, in the space available, it can focus on the critical issues central to marketing a service business on an on-going basis.

Though many specialist books currently exist on customer service, promotion, pricing theory etc[5] up until this book, there was nothing under one cover that addressed the unique components central to running a service business such as:

- Intangibility
- Process
- Resources/Capacity
- The five 'Flavors of Time'
- Customer/Market Information Systems.

Nor was there one comprehensive text addressing what they are, why they are important and how to manage them to the advantage of the business. Even so, from experience there is much more to this discipline than we can cover in the space available. Thus, we have focused on the essentials that are not adequately covered elsewhere.

References

1 *The author of such books as 'Knock Your Socks Off Service' and 'Service America'.*

2 *For example, helping the customer to purchase via such strategies as finance, counter trade and offsets.*

3 *Consumer demand drives all 'value chains' but one – defense.*

4 *If that is not the case, we recommend the precursor to this text, 'Mastering Marketing,' Ian Ruskin-Brown, Thorogood, 1999.*

5 *Skills not unique to a service business.*

ONE

Why service?

ONE
Why service? Fostering the firm's most valuable asset

Introduction

"... because services are not just valuable in there own right, they are the source of much of the (added) value in the manufacturing sector today..."

Forbes Magazine

This chapter sets out to examine the major issue underlying services marketing today, managing the relationship that a firm has with its customers, its most valuable asset. This is true whether the 'product' is a pure service, or a combination of goods and a service. The key questions that the service marketer must address are outlined, these being "Who is our target customer?" – "What is their value to us?" – "What typically do they buy?" – and "How do they judge quality, specifically our competitive edge?"

The 'relationship concept'

Whatever the business, it is important that the valuable assets of the firm are recognized as such. Indeed, if the business is a public company, the directors' first Fiduciary Duty under Company Law is often 'To Protect the Value of the Shareholder's Investment'. And, as in the 'Parable of the Talents', assets are not for burying in the ground. The job of management is to put assets to work so that their value may increase.

But what is the most valuable asset? This surely will deserve the most skillful husbanding.

The view that a firm's most valuable asset is its customer base, as is expressed in the observation that "No customers – no business" is difficult to refute, but when a firm's main 'product' is a service, it has to be more than that.

When managers in a service related business are asked to indicate their most valuable asset, the majority will reply that it is their employees, i.e. those people who run the firm.

When asked, "which particular people?" opinions will diverge. Some citing 'everyone', others the 'experts,' i.e. the guardians of the intellectual property, which, if your firm is at that end of the service spectrum (see Chapter 3) is a reasonable proposition.

It can't be denied that 'people' are a valuable asset in the service sector, service is a people business. In the classical manufacturing firm, producing and supplying goods, probably less than 10% of the people in the firm would ever meet a customer in the normal course of their job. However, if service is a major element of the business the mirror image often holds true, in that 90% of those employed will be in contact with customers in the normal course of their work, even if only by telephone.

We hold that both perspectives are right – but not quite

Because, as you, the reader, will learn:

- services are performed, not produced, and
- the delivery of this service 'performance' is critical because
- the customer 'consumes' the service as it is performed, and at the same time the customer forms:
  - an impression of its quality
  - their level of satisfaction, and
  - the basis on which they will, or will not buy from you again.

Some service authorities see this as so critical that they refer to the 'performance' occasion as *'The Moment of Truth'*, i.e. that point in time which decides the fate of the firm, at least with that customer.

Although it is people who deliver this performance to customers, both customers and servers are active participants in the process (see Chapter 8). During these 'moments of truth' the major emphasis must be to convince your customer that they have made the right choice in selecting your firm with whom to do business.

Customers should be so convinced that, at the very least, they would return to buy again from you when they are next in the market.

Ideally they should be so pleased that they recommend your firm to others (who have the potential to be customers too).

The aim, therefore, must be to build a positive long-term relationship with every customer.

By and large, relationships exist between people, not between companies or between people and companies.

This 'most valuable asset' therefore exists between your customers and those who look after your customers directly.

However, to do their job as best they can, those in direct contact with the outside customer depend on people within their own firm to provide them with the support to serve these outside customers. Such internal help is needed from among others, systems, finance, logistics, and administration. Thus, even though these support providers may rarely (if ever) meet your customers, their role in the process is critical.

Thus, in the service sector there are only two types of people:

- those who look after customers, and
- those who support the staff who look after customer.

Anyone else is a passenger (we examine this during Chapter 6).

This portfolio of relationships is the most valuable asset the firm has, and it exists between your people and the customer, or not at all and for certain types of service this is a major concern.

In addition, here are different types and strengths of relationships between the outside customer and the people within the firm who look after them. These differences are well expressed in the model known as the Ladder of Loyalty – following.

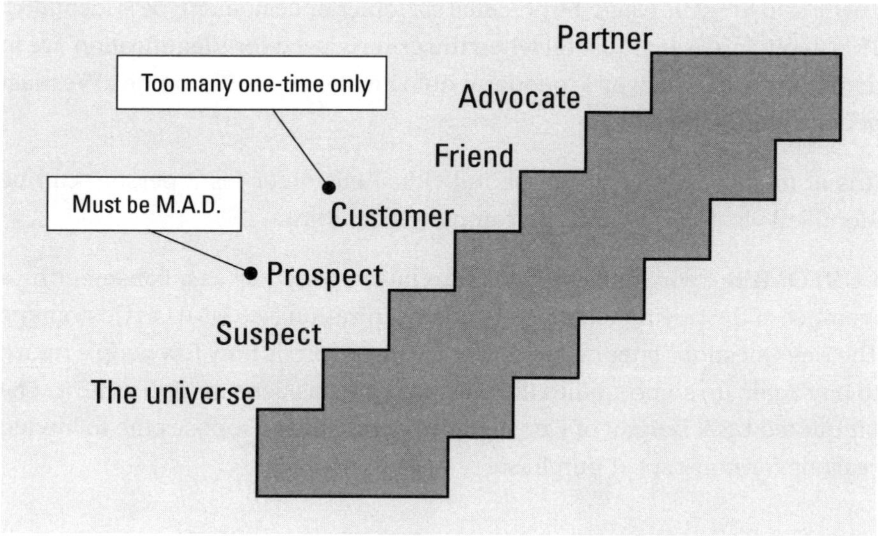

1.1: THE LADDER OF LOYALTY
(MAD = Money, Authority, Desire)

This model, suggested by Technical Assistance Research Projects Inc. (TARP) an American (USA) organization, labels the stages of gaining and retaining customers.

UNIVERSE – this is the pool from which all customers are eventually drawn. Some people and/or firms within this pool do not have the potential ever to be customers. Either they do not have the needs your 'service product' satisfies, or they may not have the ability or willingness to pay the prices you charge.

SUSPECT – this is a description of a potential customer, i.e. their characteristics. When marketing a consumer service, particularly a mass product like travel, these criteria of necessity have to be generalizations. Consumer marketers have therefore evolved a whole range of discriminatory tools like Socio Economics (SEG), Geo Demographics, and Psycho Graphics to sort the attractive from the unattractive and to focus their promotional effort where it will do the most good.

However, the more the firm moves toward addressing business-to-business markets and/or specialist consumer markets such as (say) family law and private medical health care the more the firm must be focused on its specification of how to recognize a potential customer (see Chapter 10 re. segmentation).

PROSPECT – is a person subject to the process, which is trying to persuade them to buy, i.e. to become a customer.

This is said to occur when the potential customer or customer type is identified. This 'typifying' is least useful when the criteria used for identification are in generalist terms such as a 'gender within an age and SEG[1] range'. We must get closer than that.

It is at its most useful when the individual customer (as a person) can be identified via, for example, the company's database.

CUSTOMER – someone who has purchased, whether as a consumer or a member of the buying team within an organization (see DMU in Customers: The Key Questions later in this chapter). Of concern is how few people return to buy again. In some studies the wastage rate has been as high as 92%. The oft quoted USA Bureau of Consumer Affairs[2] study proposes the following reasons for non-repeat purchase:

Died	1%
Moved away[3]	3%
Formed other affiliations	5%
Found the competitor irresistible	9%
Product dissatisfaction	14%
Encountered an 'attitude of indifference' towards them from one or more people representing the supplier"	68%

But of those who do re-buy:

The **FRIEND** – is perhaps the most numerous category of repeat customer. These 'Friends' are so valuable that accountants put them on the firm's balance sheet (how's that for respectability?). If the firm is old fashioned they are shown under 'Goodwill' – if the firm is 'modern' these customers are shown as 'Brand Equity'. When Philip Morris purchased Kraft Foods, it paid $12.5 bn. more for the firm than the book value of the tangible assets. Why? Philip Morris was paying to gain access to all those people who regularly buy Kraft products, from salad dressings to processed cheese.

It is not just their repeat purchases that makes 'Friends' valuable, the cost of replacing them can be considerable.

Studies show that on average it costs a minimum of five times as much to gain a customer as it does to persuade them to buy again and again. So for every customer who is *not lost*, the firm is in profit to the tune of at least four times the cost of looking after him or her.

However there are three other types of customer who are more valuable than 'Friends', the first of these we call:

ADVOCATES – these people tell others how wonderful we are (always assuming we have been fostering our relationships and not exhibiting 'an attitude of indifference'). Left to their own devices advocates will recommend us to at least five other 'prospects'– and it costs us nothing.

But take care, several studies have shown that the advocate's vengeance can be terrible if they are disappointed. We can do this when serving them personally (we can all have an off day). This is bad enough, remember they have recommended us to others, and poor service will put the probity of that recommendation in doubt, OR we can let down the person to whom we were recommended: now egg is all over that advocate's ego and we will be made to pay.

> It is said that:
>
> 85% of advocates will tell at least ten prospects how poor (at giving good service) we are, and that
>
> 13% will tell 20, and that
>
> the remaining 2% will go on a life's crusade against us.

It must have been advocates that Congrieve had in mind when he penned those immortal works *"Hell hath no fury like the woman scorned"*.

However, to stay positive, there are types of customer who are even more valuable than the basic advocate.

One of these is referred to as a:

PARTNER – in Relationship Marketing[4], the 'Partner' is a customer type who perceives no boundary between our firm and themselves. They believe and act as though they and we were all in the same team, on the same side, co-operating toward the common goal of good profitable business, via customer satisfaction.

This has long been part of the Japanese way of business, known there as 'Kieretsue', but within Europe such behavior is a culture shock.

The third type of 'most valuable customer', (a variant of the 'Partner') is the:

COMPLAINANT (i.e. the one who complains). These people tell us what we are doing wrong and how we can improve our customer satisfaction. Yet frequently the firm at the receiving end of this advice will dismiss it as a complaint, with a remark to the effect that 'nobody else complains'. In other words, and to our detriment, we label them as trouble-makers, rather than treat the complainant as the valuable person that they are (we examine this more closely in Chapter 11, Marketing/Customer Information).

So how does a firm in the service sector set out on this journey towards building and maintaining profitable customer relationships?

A clue to the answer to this question was provided by the very considerable study conducted by the McKinsey corporation in the 1970s, and reported by Bob Waterman and Tom Peters in their book *In Search of Excellence*.

The traits of 'excellence'

A firm is said to be 'excellent' when its customers put that firm in the top quartile of the firms they prefer to deal with (i.e. the top 25% of a list arranged in descending order of satisfaction).

There are said to be some eight factors that were identified as contributing to excellence, three of them being invariable in the top performing companies, they are:

- a focus on achieving total customer satisfaction,
- a focus on continuous innovation,

- a recognition, throughout the firm, that success in the above two factors is achieved only by a concerted effort from **all of the people** within.

We will re-visit these themes several times throughout this book: they are central to the successful marketing of a service, and service related products.

Marketing – a useful definition

There are many definitions of 'Marketing', most tell you what marketing sets out to accomplish, but few tell you how to do it. An exception, and one that is highly pertinent to the marketing of a service, is the definition proposed by Malcolm MacDonald of Cranfield University who once put it like this:

> *"Marketing is about conducting a dialogue over time with a specific group of customers whose needs you get to understand in depth and for whom you develop a specific offer with a (sustainable) differential advantage over the offers of your competitors.*
>
> He goes on to say that:
>
> *When you have something to shout about, then shout!*
>
> If not:
>
> *then shut up until you do!"*

The first statement has some key words that should be noted. Firstly, **'dialogue'**. Marketing a service – it's not a 'diatribe' with the firm talking at the customer, it is a conversation *with* the customer. The good marketer listens more than talks. The old salesman's adage applies **"God gave us two eyes,**

two ears and only one mouth", perhaps indicating the ratio in which they should be used.

The second key words are **'over time'**, indicating that this should be a continuous activity, not market research. Market research is a sporadic, expensive and highly intensive activity of short duration. It also has the unwelcome habit of annoying customers if not done with sensitivity (many people with responsibility in business today suffer from research fatigue).

The key is to use a continuous, low intensity, low cost activity which we will call a Marketing or Customer Information System (MktIS/CIS), which is part of the Management Information System (MIS) – we deal with this in Chapter 7.

The third element that deserves to be highlighted is **a specific group of customers** – no firm today can expect to achieve success by trying to be all things to all people. To build a profitable relationship we must get close to particular customers, which means that some potential customers will be ignored.

The service marketer must address this issue, and it should be clear on what basis the choice is made. Is it to be:

- long-term profit,
- market penetration,
- short-term gains,
- or what?

We look at this again below and in Chapter 10, Segmenting a service market.

Understand in depth and **differential advantage** go hand in glove.

Successful businesses in a competitive market are successful because they get closer to their customers than the competition.

This closeness translates into a more complete understanding of the customer's needs re. the 'product' (goods or service), ideally, better than the customers do themselves. This understanding provides the basis on which that business can offer that customer a 'product' which comes closest to their needs, and which they cannot get elsewhere.

The service marketer should never be satisfied with what they know about the customer. You can never know too much. However, it is worth remembering that information costs money and the service marketer should be aware that the law of diminishing returns sets in somewhere about the 80/20 rule. This means that the first (circa) 20% of information will be cheaper per quantum than the remaining 80%, and will enable the service marketer to make 80% of the key decisions; whereas the remaining 80% of information will probably not only cost more per quantum, but will probably only be of use (circa) 20% of the time.

Finally, the key factor in any relationship is to build trust; the successful service marketer does not promise what can't be delivered. They would rather 'under promise and over deliver', as we will see in Chapter 4.

Customers: The key questions

Thus, in pursuit of the firm's most valuable asset, the ('Customer Relationship'), there are some key questions which the service marketer must address, with care and skill. These are:-

Who is my typical customer?

The frequent reply to this question is that the firm has no *typical* customer. Customers are all different. Indeed, all human beings are individual, but such observations are not very useful.

In most cases the service marketer's job is to classify their prospects and customers into typologies, (such clusters are generically known as 'segments'), not to do so implies a strategy of 'one size fits all'. By grouping customers into homogeneous clusters (segments) the service marketer is able to get much closer to satisfying each customer's needs (that is both the aim and the skill).

The exception is when the firm's business is derived from a few large customers[5]. In these cases each customer may contribute such a significant share of the firm's business and each customer may be so significantly different from each other, that it is best to treat every one of them as a segment in their own right, this strategy is known as 'Key Account Management'.

Even if the firm is engaged in B2B markets, it is not helpful to classify the customer as a 'firm', a 'company', or an 'organization'. It is people who buy, not companies or markets. It is the people in those firms, companies and markets who make and execute the buying decisions.

Further, there are very few purchases which are made by the individual acting alone (and then mainly in consumer markets). It is normal human behavior to reduce risk by seeking advice and input from others. This group-buying behavior is well documented and understood: marketers of all types refer to the group of people involved as the Decision Making Unit (DMU).

The main roles, whether in business-to-business or in consumer markets, in brief are:

BUYER/S

The person/s who actually place the order, the Purchasing or Procurement Manager of an organization. The mum solo shopping for her family.

DECIDER/S

The person/s who take/s responsibility.

USER/S

The internal consumer, the worker using the commodity or equipment purchased, the stock controller.

SPECIFIER/S

The person with particular knowledge who 'specifies' the features to be purchased (sometimes the 'user').

SEARCHER/S AND GATEKEEPER/S

Person/s who control the flow of information into the DMU.

Searchers are active, they seek out the required data, Gatekeeper/s are passive, they act as a valve, permitting some information (or informants) to flow in, but keeping others out.

Examples – on the consumer side are wives and other women close to the family; on the commercial side are trainees, PAs, secretaries, design departments etc. **A very powerful role.**

RECOMMENDER/S

Person/s who advocate a supplier, they can be internal to the family or firm, or external.

INITIATOR/S

Those who provoke the buying process, they recognize the need and bring it to the attention of other members of the organization/DMU.

INFLUENCER/S

Person/s within the family or firm who bring influence to bear, though they are not a directly active part of the DMU, examples are: uncles, aunts, parents etc. or even accountants, budgeters or change agents.

VALIDATOR/S

Persons from outside the organization, opinion leaders, peer group leaders, such as media commentators and consumer groups etc.

There are also combined roles such as in the so-called USER-CHOOSER where, for example, the person who will attend an MBA course is the one who chooses at which university they will study.

Whether our service business is to the consumer direct, or via a business customer, it is vital to know what roles are played in the buying process by which individuals.

What is a customer's lifetime value?

The well considered answer to this question reinforces the sheer good business sense behind the practice of building and husbanding customer relationships for the long-term.

The principle is to calculate how much income a customer can bring to the firm over the lifetime of their commercial relationship.

There are several ways to calculate this value – here is the most straightforward:

- Take the size of an average purchase and multiply this by the expected number of that type of customer's purchases per year, then multiply this by the expected number of years of the relationship. In most businesses it is reasonable to further multiply this figure by the factor of advocates to customers in your business, (in general terms say a ratio of one advocate for every four friends producing a factor of ¼) and then by the number of prospects referred by each advocate, say five prospects per advocate.

Thus, Lifetime Value =

the average spend per year X number of expected years X 2¼ *
*[*in this case every fourth 'friend' brings in five new customers, i.e. 5 ÷ 4 = 1¼, added to the customer's 1, = 2¼]*

- So, for example, a major supermarket would calculate this way:

Average spend per household per week on groceries = £75.00

Number of weeks per year = 52 (disregard taking holidays because Christmas spending makes up for it), Expected life of relationship = 10 years.[6]

Thus the lifetime value of a supermarket customer equates to:

£75 x 52 weeks x 10 years x 2¼ = £87,750

A considerable figure.

A major supermarket is said to have used such a calculation in the early 1980s to convince institutional investors of the viability of its expansion program.

They wished to open one new out of town shopping center, per month for some eleven years. Each store was then said to cost upward of £14m.

It is perhaps no accident that, at the time of writing, the firm in question has the largest market share and is by far the most profitable supermarket in the UK.

What typically do they buy?

The successful management of any commercial 'relationship' requires that we provide the customer with an offering that more closely meets their needs than the competitors.

Customers rarely buy what we sell; they buy what they get out of what we sell them. As any proficient professional salesperson will confirm, we provide features, the customers buy benefits (see the section on the 'Levitt Construct' Chapter 5).

The service marketer must therefore take care to view the 'service product' from the same perspective as the customer: 'What are the customer's needs? What are the benefits required?' We must resist the temptation to see the 'service product' from our internal perspective.

Each member of the DMU will have their own fairly unique perspective. Take as an example the provision of a training service.

The Decider may be the trainee's departmental head, not their immediate boss, and the Decider may view the training as a way of rewarding the boss and the trainee.

A major Influencer could be the Financial Director, and their need is to manage budgets more closely.

The trainer's boss could be **the Specifier**, trying to ensure an improvement in departmental productivity, and satisfy a need to show the departmental head that action is being taken.

The User is the trainee, perhaps with an eye to improving their market value, etc. The main message from this is that the service marketer needs to be sensitive to these nuances, and to communicate accordingly.

The Validators could be peers to any of these people and/or an external body such as OMTRACK[7].

In addition, each of the segments will have unique needs, as exemplified by the differing views expressed in recent advertising campaigns for pension products (financial services), each for different target groups[8]. Whilst one major pension company, with its tag line 'Grow old disgracefully', saw the pension as a vehicle whereby its TG could 'self actualize' (i.e. do all those interesting and exciting things customers had no time to do whilst they were busy earning a living), another saw the pension as a step-up from the subsistence of the state scheme with its tag of "Who could live off £3,000 pa. nowadays?"

(See Chapter 10, Segmenting a service market.)

How do customers judge quality?

The successful service marketer will not just meet the customer's needs, but in addition they will delight the customer by exceeding expectations. This can be expressed as either one of two equations:

SATISFACTION = PERCEPTION *minus* EXPECTATIONS.

When perceptions are greater than expectations, the customer is delighted, but when perceptions are less than expected, the customer is disappointed. **OR** as suggested by Malcolm Macdonald:

$$\text{Perceived Value} = \frac{\text{Perceived Relative Benefit (PRB)}^{9}}{\text{Perceived Relative Cost (PRC)}}$$

When value is greater than 'One' *(i.e. PRB > PRC)* the customer is delighted, and the service marketer can (almost) be assured the customer will return (i.e. the probability of re-buy is c.90%).

However, if value is less than 'One' *(i.e. PRB < PRC)* the customer is disappointed and frequently there will be no repeat purchase (here the probability of re-buy is c.40%).

Whichever equation we use, it is amazing how little it takes to tip the balance either way.

For example, a restaurant that is only 'satisfactory' can create delight when the owner recognizes people by name as a regular customer or, on departure, presents the ladies in the party with some token of thanks, a flower say; alternatively an otherwise perfect restaurant experience could be totally ruined on the discovery of a soiled item of cutlery.

Two things arise from this:

> *"What will cause delight?"*
>
> **and**
>
> *"Can this be depended on to always do so?"*

In the first case it depends on the needs of the person concerned. Take for instance the case of how a family may evaluate their bathroom facilities.

For a large family, of say four children, all of whom are active and frequently get their clothes and themselves dirty, a major evaluative criteria could probably be plenty of hot water and lots of warm towels.

However, for a couple next door, whose main leisure activity is entertaining friends to dinner, their criteria for satisfaction may be that the bathroom should be attractively furnished (e.g. a bidet, gold taps throughout etc.) so they don't feel embarrassed by it when their house guests come to call.

It can be seen from both the bathroom examples that once the current criteria are satisfied, then the factors that satisfy are taken for granted and become the 'expected'.

So, for the restaurant, the flower is soon taken for granted, it becomes the norm, and guests become bored rather than delighted. Now something new, unexpected must be provided to cause delight. The risk is that for each subsequent visit the novelty item must outdo the previous one. First it becomes a bunch of flowers, and when that pales, a box of chocolates, and next a small bottle of 'complimentary' dessert wine, and so it goes on. Eventually the proprietor will either be giving away the profits or have to raise prices and/or the cover charge to make up the loss.

The key is to do something 'surprising' as a normal part of the business. Perhaps the restaurateur could run a promotion that guaranteed that the ladies in a party will always be presented with a different flower from the one they were given last time, or a free bottle of Champagne if the restaurant gets it wrong (the author has heard of a restaurant where this is said to work well, engendering a great deal of word of mouth publicity).

In the case of the bathroom, when the children are grown and gone, the parents criteria for satisfaction will probably change to be more like their neighbors next door.

The issue is for the service provider to address those things that the customer values, rather than to add to the specification for the sake of it. This is the difference between luxury and quality. What is important to the customer is called 'salient', and the issue of how we gain the insight into what is salient and for whom, is explained in Chapter 13, Seriously seeking feedback.

In business-to-business markets it is not so easy to get close to the customer, it takes time – except for a few types of the very smallest of firms who have become very savvy at buying. That, after all, is all there is to business:

a) buying well, perhaps adding value (lowest possible cost, highest possible value) and

b) selling well (highest possible price).

If b) is greater than a), they make a profit and survive to do it again, if not they soon go under.

SO, the business customer will be wary before accepting that the supplier has good intentions. Even so, as research shows, there are only certain circumstances where the business customer will want to get into a partnership with the seller; e.g. where what the seller provides is of critical importance to the customer's business, AND it is either in short supply AND/OR the buying firm spends lots of money on the products in question.[10]

In most other permutations of these criteria the business customer will benefit from maintaining distance and playing the various suppliers off against each other. In these situations the seller must add value, usually via 'service' along the lines of the Levitt Construct (Chapter 5.)

However, even assuming that the customer can see an advantage in getting closer to the seller, the customer will be cautious and will only be won over via a 'courtship' which will take time and effort from the seller to ensure success.

These courtships will go through several stages, during which the seller has to lead and the customer has to be convinced before progressing to the next stage (does this sound familiar?). We see this courtship dance plotted in Figure 1.2 following.

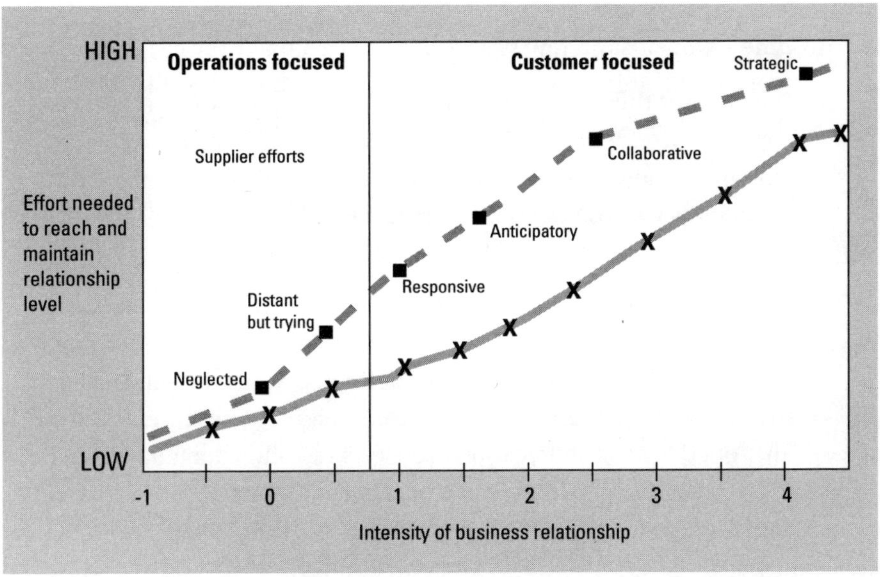

1.2: CUSTOMER SERVICE, CUSTOMER FOCUS – KEY TO SUCCESS

The vertical axis shows the amount of effort each party puts into the courtship, the horizontal axis shows the intensity of the relationship – from mutual neglect through to a strategic partnership.

In the early stages, whilst the relationship can best be described as 'operations focused' (i.e. the whole thing can be seen as pure logistics, something similar to accessing supply on the Web alone) the supplier has to do all the 'courting' – the customer is not convinced there is any point in getting closer.

IF the supplier is sensitive to the customer's real needs, and is applying this insight by responding to them, then there will eventually be a tentative response from the customer.

Later the supplier aims to anticipate the customers needs which will then encourage the customer to get closer and open-up to, and collaborate with the service provider in an effort to have their supplies more 'customized' still.

Eventually, if all goes well, the service is so tailored to the customer's needs that they are getting unique value from this supplier, and the relationship is seen as being strategic. The product surround (see Chapter 5) mainly consisting of 'services', from stock management, through financing, and partnership pricing to market development, has become the real source of value. The 'generic' product, so often in reality a commodity good, has become merely the means by which this valued service is paid for.

Two examples serve to illustrate:

1 The hero of this story is a major telecommunications equipment supplier (who will remain anonymous). As well as handsets for example, they sell the heavy equipment that goes into the exchanges via which mobile telephone calls are routed. These are known as 'switches' and they cost a lot of money.

The mobile telecommunications companies who buy and use these 'switches' are known as 'operators', most countries now have several operators providing competing services and because of the competition, and the way that many governments have auctioned telecommunication licenses, they often don't have much spare cash lying around so the purchase of switches is very price sensitive.

The technology is such that one manufacturer's switches are very much like any other. However, whereas most of the competition compete on price, our heroes have set up a totally unique service whereby they never actually sell the equipment to customers. They 'lend' it to their customers, install it, train the customer's people to run it, maintain it for the customer, upgrade hardware and software as and when necessary, give customers market advice gained from their experience with other operators elsewhere in the world, help them anticipate trends for mobile usage for the various markets that may be served by an operator etc.

And for recompense, our heroes are paid a share of the operator's income, monthly and in arrears.

All of which are ways of adding value via service 'products'.

And the proof of this pudding is that at the time of writing, whilst nearly all of the competition were in dire economic circumstances, our heroes were the top selling and most profitable telecommunications equipment manufacturer in the world.

The second illustration relates to tyres.

2. The firm in point is called 'The Classic Connection' and they supply the tyres for vintage and classic cars and motorcycles, to wealthy collectors and museums throughout the world.

   Their main 'product' is knowing which tyres go on what vehicles, and where these tyres can be sourced.

   However, to their customers, what makes them attractive is that they will often deliver and fit these tyres personally, thus ensuring that this expensive purchase has been properly installed.

   The Classic Connection sells tyres, but customers buy, and pay handsomely for, the service.

Exercise

Thinking about your business:

1. What is the (modal) average of the lifetime value of your customers to your business?
2. How would you describe your target group of 'potential customers'?
3. Name three 'friends', i.e. regular customers. Those who repeat buy, and have done so for some time now.
4. What proportion of your business consists of customers who you only ever serve once, then you never see them again?
   - Is this normal, or is there something you could do to make more of them repeat customers? If so:
   - What do you intend to do?
5. Name one 'advocate' and identify how many 'customers' you believe they have recommended to your business.
   - How many other advocates could you (or your people in the front-line) name?
   - Are you satisfied that you know them all?
   - Are you satisfied with this number of advocates?

6. How many times over the last year have you listened to customer complaints?
   - How many of these did you seek out, and how many came to you unprompted?
   - What proportion did these form of the total possible complaints?
   - Assuming you can't say how many causes for complaints there could have been, what are you going to do to find this out in future?
   - Of those complaints you listened to, what have you done to ensure that the causes of them do not happen again?

References

1 *Socio-Economic Group.*

2 *Also attributed to the Rockefeller Corporation Study reported in the US News and World Report article 'Your cheque is in the post'.*

3 *NB. Either physically moved out of the locality, or 'matured' out of the market, as would be the case when (as per Private Education) the children are no longer of school age (though this does not mean that they may not return when the offspring have children of their own).*

4 *Sometimes referred to as Customer Relationship Marketing (CRM).*

5 *Typical of B2B (Business-to-Business) markets.*

6 *The main reason people now change their 'out of town shopping center' stores, is said to be when they move house. We are said to be unwilling to travel more than 12 mins. on average to get to our favorite stores.*

7 *An independent validating body for the various training bodies.*

8 *N.B. Often shortened to 'TG' and another way of saying which segment is being addressed, and for whom within that segment, the communication is intended.*

9 *N.B. 'Perceived Cost' is everything involved in obtaining the service, not just price, but including the trouble of searching for a supplier, and any involvement they may have in obtaining the benefits, e.g. learning the software etc. Whereas 'Perceived Benefit' is a little more difficult to assess, and may often have to employ sophisticated Market Research tools such as 'Trade-Off Analysis' (conjoint analysis) etc. See Pricing.*

10 *A small percentage improvement in the cost of buying can have an enormous effect on the bottom line of the firm. 'See Key Account Management' Peter Cheverton, published by Kogan Page; or 'Key Account Management' by Professor Malcolm McDonald, published by Butterworth Heinemann.*

TWO

What is a service?

TWO
What is a service?

Introduction

"Luncheons 12pm – 3pm, seductions 7pm onward."

(Sign on the author's favorite bistro in Kensington, circa 1960's)

This chapter takes a 'Cook's Tour' around the essential of what differentiates a service from a good, and then proceeds with an overview of how, in order to address these differences, the marketing mix for a service must be extended beyond the conventional so called 4 x Ps of Product, Price, Promotion and Place. Thus, to exploit the strengths and opportunities and to address the weaknesses and threats inherent in a service business.

The characteristics that differentiate a service

For a marketer, the best way to describe a service is to describe how it differs from a 'good'.

In no particular order of importance, *(this order will change with circumstances),* we set out below these commonly accepted differences, firstly as topics, following which each is explained in turn:

A service is characterized by being:

- **Intangible**
- **Performed**

- **Perishable**
- **People dominated**
- **No ownership of the resource used by the customer – and**
- **Copyable, i.e. there is little if any ownership of the idea**
- **No second-hand resale value**
- **Enabling**
- **Impossible to sample**
- **Open to 'inter-customer' influence.**

To explain:

INTANGIBLE (i.e. a service has no physical presence)

Services are predominantly intangible. A useful definition of a service compared to a 'good' is that the intangible elements of what are performed, form the greater part of what is important to the customer. It is conventional to arrange goods and services into a 'continuum' so that commodity goods such as metal ores, crude oil and other basic extracted goods are at the one end, and pure intellectual property based services such as training, professional advice, the law and consultancy are at the other. This is shown in Fig 2.1. It will be seen that even though the commodity goods are basic, frequently they can have associations with the intangible, Solingen Iron Ore for the best quality blades, Saudi Crude for the sweetest emissions (*i.e. no sulphurous fumes*). Indeed many marketers of commodity goods have employed brand strategies where the intangibles are the differentiator: *"In the factory we make cosmetics, in the shop we sell hope"*[11].

Below we see a diagram representing this continuum.

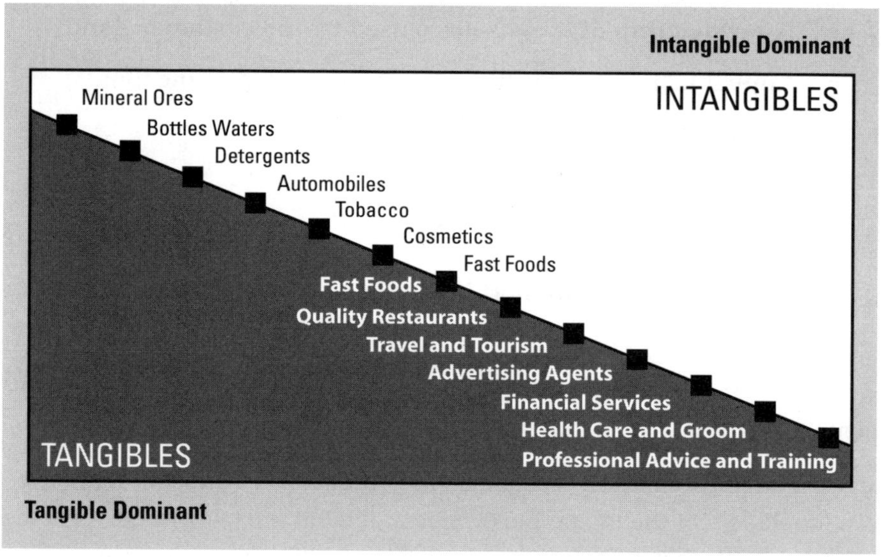

FIG 2.1: THE GOODS AND SERVICES CONTINUUM

At the watershed where the intangible process (see the next issue below) and tangible goods are of the same proportion the product becomes a service for our purposes, and the further to the right on this continuum, the greater the importance of the intangible performance. This part of a service (i.e. what is performed for the customer) cannot be touched, tasted, weighed or its length measured. The customer cannot have a smooth, rough, hot or cold service, nor can they have it in any color. This intangibility means that the customer's assessment of **the quality of any service must therefore be based on subjective criteria**, and the more the service product is located toward the right of the continuum, the more subjective must their judgment be. Restaurants, airlines, car hire firms, hotels, all have physical things which are intrinsic to the service provided, but for services such as the law, auditing, training, etc. the tangibles must be provided, they are not naturally present in the nature of the service (see Chapter 7).

The service marketer must address this aspect of intangibility, because everywhere the customer comes into contact with their service, they will be hungry for clues as to the quality of the service provided. This is a search for reassurance that they have done the right thing in choosing a particular provider. If unrequited, this search can prove dangerous to the firm's relationship with the customer (and will lead to 'cognitive dissonance', an irritant which provokes dissatisfaction). So the service marketer must provide something to 'tangible-ise' the service product. (We examine this further in Chapter 7.)

However, to successfully market a service, the most obvious issues are not always the most useful. The marketer has to look a little deeper for clues as to how best these different characteristics should be addressed to build the service business more effectively.

PERFORMED (not produced)

Services are performed; they are not produced. From serving at table, to making a plea in court, in the sense that the service is a deed being conducted (for the customer) at a given point in time, **it is all a performance!**

The 'real time' nature of the performance also means that a service is highly flexible. At best it can be tailored to suit the particular customer being served. At worst there is the danger of a wide variation in delivery leading to difficulties in quality control, and also lack of a consistent identity across service deliverers and outlets. The service marketer must manage this variability to advantage via the use of action standards and evaluation systems. (This is dealt with more comprehensively in Chapter 4.)

PERISHABLE (a service is transient, it has no shelf life)

A result of the performance aspect is that a service is perishable... yesterday's service is gone forever; the service marketer can only sell what service can be provided from now onward. A hotel that failed to book all its rooms last night has lost that potential income completely, no matter how high the demand today, they can only book the rooms available today.

Neither can a service be produced from stock. Take an extreme example of a hair salon. In anticipation of the strong demand for their services on Saturday, the hairdressers cannot produce haircuts for stock on Thursday – and on Saturday greet the 'un-booked' customers, Blue Peter style, with: "Ah Mrs. Jones, I know we are busy but here is one we did earlier".

This example points out a further result of the 'performance' nature of services, the production of any service is inseparable from its consumption.

Production and consumption occur simultaneously.

The above have many important implications for the marketing of a service, and Chapter 4 is devoted to an examination of this performance in so far as it can contribute toward the marketing strategy, planning, and operations of the firm providing a 'service product'.

PEOPLE DOMINATED

"Service is adding people to the product"

Ron Zemke

The performance mentioned above is carried out via the people in the firm, all of them, not just those in the front-line (ref. the internal and external customer in Chapter 6). If there are no people involved, such as in the case of Automatic Teller Machines [ATMs] to be found in the walls of the branches of banks and building societies, or automatic telephone receptions ("Your call is important to us (who is kidding who?), please hold, you are number nine in the queue") then, in the view of this author, that is not a service, it is a facility, and its marketing should take this into account.

Services are 'inseparable' from the people who provide them, and because people are individuals, each one uniquely different from their neighbor, the service marketing strategy must address this variation, (frequently referred to as 'Heterogeneity' – which is sometimes a strength, and sometimes a weakness; we examine this in Chapter 6).

NO OWNERSHIP OF THE RESOURCE USED

Frequently the service customer buys the right to use resources over time. For example, the hotel bedroom, the hire car, the airplane seat, the restaurant's chairs, table, cutlery, crockery. But these do not belong to the customer. After the agreed time span or its equivalent, e.g. when the plane arrives at the destination, the meal is consumed etc., they must be returned to the ownership of the service provider.

COPYABLE (difficult to 'own' the idea)

A service may not be patented; there are very few ways in which a service marketer can protect the new service idea from being emulated. Indeed one of the first indications that the service marketer may have a success on their hands is when the competition copies it. This issue needs to be addressed with care. (We examine how during Chapter 5.)

NO RESALE VALUE (no second-hand market)

There is 'futures value' only, but very little 'residual value' (if any) in a service.

RESIDUAL VALUE

No one would want to buy the haircut the reader may have recently been given. A barrister's advice to a given client is situation specific, and could not, with confidence, be sold to another person by that client.

FUTURES VALUE

This is to do with the need for some services to load their capacity early, as is the case, either of a scheduled airline on a not too popular route, or of a freelance trainer in marketing. The airline has to sell a good tranche of the seats on a given flight (day, time and destination) as early as possible, which means that these sales may have to be at concessionary prices (Apex etc. direct to passengers or via 'bucket-shops'), in order to guarantee the economic viability of that flight. The professional trainer has similarly to guarantee the economics of a given year by selling advanced loading at concessionary rates in order to break-even.

In both cases, once 'break-even' is reached, then the emphasis on pricing will be to produce the best profit. (We look at this in more detail in Chapter 12, Pricing a service business.)

ENABLING (the prime function of any service)

A service will enable the customer to obtain the benefits they seek. A pension plan will provide security in old age; a holiday package will enable rest and recuperation, etc.

Where the service is used to add value to a good, this 'enabling' may often be the main way in which the benefits are provided, for example, a personal computer for the home office is just a hunk of metal, silicone and plastic without the installation, training and hotline support most people need.

All products (goods or services) enable benefits to be obtained, this is not unique to services. However, in a way similar to the Tangible vs. Intangible ratio seen earlier it is critical to them. Enablement is the services' raison d'être, a fact frequently forgotten in such sectors as financial services.

A SERVICE CANNOT BE SAMPLED

A prospect cannot sample a haircut, a solicitor's advice, a holiday, a pension plan, they either consume these services, albeit in smaller quantities, one haircut, a quarter of an hour's legal advice, a weekend away, etc. (what can be done in the case of a pension?) or they do not.

Mostly therefore, up until the moment of the service's performance, it is all 'promise'. However, inter-customer influence can be a surrogate for sampling.

INTER-CUSTOMER INFLUENCE (who else is being served by that provider?)

The prospect may not be able to sample a pension et al but they can talk to people who have (*and have experienced delivery of*) any of the above examples. They can thus discover if these customers were satisfied, and form an opinion of how likely it is that they too will be satisfied.

The use of 'reference sites' where prospects can see the service in use and talk to the customers is highly recommended – as is skillfully used in corporate hospitality, and exploiting the firm's client lists (see Chapter 11).

Some types of service are delivered in a social context. For these the management of how one customer may be affected by, or may affect other customers, is an important aspect for the service marketer to manage.

THE SERVICE SPECTRUM

A useful model here is the 'Services Spectrum' shown below.

Most of these are either service providers in their own right, or they are bundled in with goods to add value to the tangible part of the product and thus add a 'competitive edge'. Services to the bottom right are the most likely to be used this way.

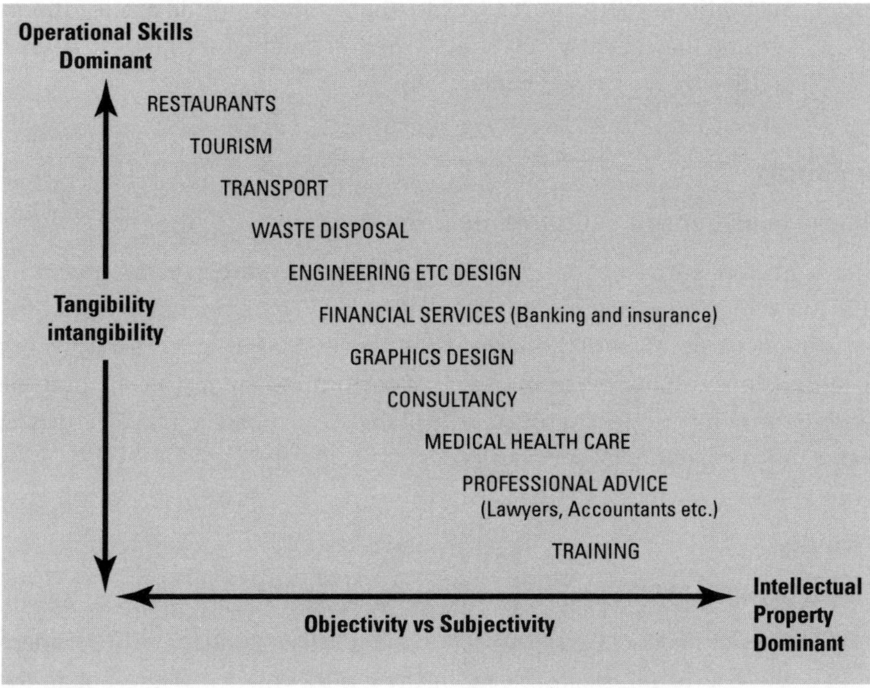

FIG 2.2: THE SERVICES SPECTRUM

There are many types of service; they range from fast-food and restaurants through to professional advice. There are also several perspectives via which a service can be classified – we will examine each in turn.

The main points to be noted from the Services Spectrum are:

Firstly

The balance between Manual Skills vs. Intellectual Content.

- At the top left of the spectrum, the service is dominated by operational skills, it is mainly the performance of a manual skill of some kind, cooking, serving at table, nursing, chiropody etc. This is not to say that there are no intellectual skills involved, far from it, but these are in support of the manual task which is physical.
- Whilst at the bottom right of the spectrum the situation is reversed. The service is mainly about what the practitioner knows, their intellectual property. Though many practitioners at this end of the spectrum are in the 'Professions', manual skills are frequently involved,

such as in: surgery, court advocacy (public speaking), data entry, report writing (particularly nowadays when so much of the keyboard work is done by the person concerned).

Secondly

Where management skills are most required.

Although there are exceptions, notably restaurants at one end of the spectrum, and the provision of training at the other end. The amount to which the performance/operation of the service (the process) will require management co-ordination and support from those not performing the service themselves, tends to be at its greatest in the middle of the spectrum, e.g. travel, tourism, waste disposal, financial services etc.

Thirdly

The degree to which quality can be judged 'objectively'.

- Service products to the top left of the spectrum tend to be those where the use of physical objects in their performance is the norm, for example:
  - Restaurants – food, crockery, cutlery, furniture, etc.
  - Airlines – airplanes, check-in desks, ticketing etc.
  - Nursing – thermometers, bandages, pills & potions etc.

Whilst the physical accompaniments of service performed at the bottom right of the spectrum tend to be there more for psychological reasons (designed specifically to directly affect the participant's perception), for example:

- The law, barristers, judges, clerks of the court etc. (wigs, gowns, the Judge's Bench).
- Advertising industry, their offices – location and decor, cars, dress, literature etc.
- Accountancy, as above.

It is also interesting to note that where practitioners see themselves located on this Services Spectrum tends to change according to how customers are referred to. It ranges from 'customers' at the top left (the exceptions including medical care) to 'clients' at the bottom right. This difference in perspective tends to affect the way the 'customer' is treated. If seen as a 'customer', the practitioner tends to have little inhibitions about getting close to that person; actual (as opposed to effected) friendship with customers can be part of building the business. Whilst, if seen as a 'client', friendship is taboo, even though 'friendliness' is a necessary skill of the 'professional' practitioner.

Of necessity, in these types of business, there is a need to maintain a distance between the service provider, and the 'client' (An axiom of the legal professions has it that "one should never make a client of a friend, or a friend of a client".)

The extended service mix

To paraphrase David Jobber[12]:

"whilst it is possible to discuss the marketing mix for a service within the 4 x Ps framework of Product, Placement, Promotion and Price (Physical Evidence, Process, etc. can be considered as part of the 'Product'), the use of the extended mix allows a more thorough analysis of the ingredients necessary for successful services marketing".

This nicely describes the author's opinion and it is his experience that the marketing of a service can only be improved when all aspects of the extended mix are understood and addressed. Much of the failure of service firms to reach their full potential, (in terms of long-term customer relationships and subsequent profit optimization), can be attributed to a lack of understanding of the workings of the various elements of the extended mix. And in consequence a lack of actions that address these factors effectively.

This is particularly true in the United Kingdom. In those sectors of the service industry which are facing increasing competition, the emphasis is too often on operations orientation (the service business's version of 'product orientation') or on sales orientation, as though cost control and forceful persuasion held all the answers.

As Tom Peters puts it:

"You only have to do it right and you will succeed, because you will have no competition."

So the remainder of this chapter will provide a quick introduction to this extended mix, relating each element to the relevant differences between goods and services, as we have discussed above.

In order of importance, AND IN ADDITION TO THE 4 x P's, the extra elements of the extended mix are:

PROCESS

This relates to the fact that services are performed, and consumed simultaneously (*the so-called 'Moments of Truth' the MoT*[13]).

They are not produced, nor have any shelf life.

Service is an experience and therefore the essence of the concept of PROCESS is to manage the customer's experience at the point of delivery, to control the MoT to the service provider's best advantage.

The two major components of PROCESS are 'procedures' and 'people' (sometimes referred to as 'systems' and 'smiles' respectively). Chapter 4 examines this aspect in some depth.

PEOPLE

This is a critical element of the mix for the service provider because service is 'adding people to the product', it begins with the selection of people with the right aptitudes, skills and attitudes and proceeds to policies for their empowerment, training, motivation and control. (Chapters 6 examines this aspect).

PHYSICAL EVIDENCE

This aspect of the extended mix addresses the fact that the performance of a service is intrinsically intangible. The customer will associate the physical accoutrements of that service, whether they are deliberately managed or not, with the service being provided at that place and time. It is therefore important that the service marketer should take charge of these tangibles and manage them to communicate to the customer, the required impression and image. (Chapter 7 examines this aspect.)

TIME

This element of the extended mix addresses the only 'objective' dimension on which the quality of a service can be judged. As will be seen (Chapter 10) it comes in five 'flavours' any one or a combination of which can be used to gain considerable competitive advantage.

These are:

- Punctuality,
- Availability (of the service MoT)
- Duration
- Speed of response, and
- Speed of innovation.

RESOURCE

This element has been likened to the cement that holds the other eight elements of the mix together.

Because:

- service is performed and consumed at the same time,
- it has no shelf life,

and it follows that:

- the performance of the service will be resource dependent, be these resources 'people', 'computers', 'cars', 'hotel beds', 'seats' on an airplane or whatever is employed to provide the service capacity.

Whilst it is also a fact of life that:

- customer demand fluctuates from one moment to the next, as may resource availability.

The service provider, therefore must create and adopt strategies and policies to ensure that their business is always able to optimize the match between demand and resource capacity in such a way as to avoid either:

- losing valuable customers because of poor service at times of peak demand, or

- the business bleeding to death with unused expensive spare capacity during times of slack demand.

This aspect calls for as much creativity and innovation as any other aspect of the services marketing process (see Chapter 9).

Exercise

In the context of the whole of chapter two, but with specific reference to the five elements of the Extended Marketing Mix for services as just introduced, for your Service set out what is done to address each of the mix elements. That is to say, in terms of your service business, what:

- 'Process' is involved in the delivery of your service product?
- People are employed to deliver your service, and of what general quality are they?
- Physical evidence/tangibles, with which your customers/clients come into contact, are associated with the delivery of your service?
- Are the 'flavours' of time involved in the provision of your service?
- Resources are critical to the delivery/performance of your service product?

How often do you find that either:

- A resource shortage is damaging the quality of your service delivery – or constraining how much you can deliver, or
- A surplus of resources to requirements is tying up precious money unproductively?

On each of the above five elements, score (out of 20) how well you think your service business currently performs.

- If your score is less than 60, what do you intend to do about it?
- If your score is 85 or more, look again – be more critical.

In either case – read on – there is much to learn.

References

11 *Variously attributed, but the author prefers to believe that it was Helena Rubenstein, if she did not say it, she should have.*

12 *'The Principles and Practices of Marketing', McGraw Hill 1995*

13 *'Moments of Truth – ref. The Service Blueprint in Chapter 8*

THREE

The why and where of service

THREE

The why and where of service

Introduction

"...whatever it was that got us to where we are today, is not going to be sufficient to keep us there!"

(Tony Thacker, Marcus Bohn Associates)

This chapter examines and identifies the different types of service in terms of the balance between the operational skills and the intellectual content required. It also addresses the issue of the 'objectivity' versus the 'subjectivity' content, where it is the WHOLE as opposed to the MAIN PART of the service product. The chapter concludes by examining the various services that can be used to add value, and which of these attract a fee, and which are of strategic importance.

The service spectrum: Classifying a service

The first, which we will refer to throughout this book, is the so-called 'Services Spectrum'. *See page 35, Figure 2.2.*

The proportion of 'service' in the 'product'

The service marketer will also find it useful to know where the emphasis of their 'service product' lies in terms of what proportion of the whole is 'pure service' (i.e. is intangible, is performed) and what part is a 'good' or 'goods' (i.e. is tangible, is produced). These proportions will affect the parameters within, and the means via which the 'service product' can be positioned.

Service IS THE WHOLE product

Examples of this are:

- Professional advice: accountants, solicitors, insurance;
- Training in initial, continuous, or further skills etc.
- Care and grooming services: hairdressing, chiropody, nursing;
- Transport and tourism.

In these types of service the emphasis is on the 'performance' by the individual or individuals delivering the service for the customer. As indicated in Chapter 2, the management of this performance is critical. However, the tangible elements associated with the service are of concern as well.

For the first two categories above, most, if not all, of the service can be provided without anything tangible having to be associated with the process. Of course that depends on the type of training provided, if it is 'tool based', the tangibility is of the tools themselves. Or in another example, for the barrister, the tangibles of the courtroom are a given, but are outside the advocate's control.

For these categories of 'service product' it is imperative to provide some 'physical evidence'[14], and to ensure that, whatever is associated (by accident or design), is congruent with the quality position that the service marketer wishes to communicate.

The trainer who wishes to be perceived as up-to-date and at the top end of the market will use a high specification LCD Projector with the material on a professional software package such as PowerPoint, salubrious locations for the venue, ensuring clean and well laid out training room, will dress well and drive a status car etc. etc.

(Many organizations that run training frequently ignore the issues of venue, quality and layout and too many hotels that purport to offer conference and

training facilities, will provide the most second rate equipment, often old, nearly always dirty, and too frequently damaged in a way that will lower the quality of the presentation. What is worse, they will take exception if these shortcomings are brought to their attention.)

The barrister will ensure client meetings are held in well appointed chambers, will wear a smart outfit when not in court, and when in court, will ensure that although the wig and gown are the outer garments, no frayed cuff, or soiled shirt/blouse collar shows. (This may sound obvious but, in the course of consultancy, the author has sometimes encountered counsel who have not bothered to wear clean and well repaired shirts, not realizing the affect it has on the client's perception of the professionalism and competence of that barrister[15].)

Service is THE VITAL ELEMENT of the product

Examples of this case are:

- Restaurants, and most of the rest of the hospitality sector,
- Personal computers, and much else in the IT sector,
- Finance: banking, building societies, insurance brokers, etc. etc.

In terms of the relationship of the 'service' part to the tangible aspects of the product, this category is the mirror image of the last barrister or a trainer. Here, service businesses are in danger of being distracted by the tangible items, and of neglecting the intangible process.

Banks and other financial establishments have traditionally used substantial branch buildings[16], which, by their very nature tend to be impressive edifices. This was because of the banking business, its security requirements, and the need to impress customers with the safe and substantial nature of the business (they are not about to disappear with your savings overnight – one hopes). In addition, it is not uncommon for branch staff to look on the physical money as a 'good'.

Restaurants can get 'hooked' into the physicality of the food, its presentation in particular, the host of tangibles that go to create the ambience. After all most people do not often visit restaurants just to get a square meal, they go for the totality of the experience. A fact recognized in the extreme by the 'theme' restaurant, such as Planet Hollywood and TGI Friday at the one end of the scale, and Le Manoir Aux Quatre Saison, at the other. This distraction can, between these extremes, cause the firm to neglect that their business is a service. This neglect being manifest by hiring too few staff, often of indifferent quality, and rarely trained either by the business, the industry or previous attendance at relevant colleges.

The humble personal computer (PC) is a prime example of the total product being a meld of the service and good. By itself the PC is a useless lump of plastic, silicone, rubber et al. It is only when the service side is present that it has any utility other than acting as office décor. It is the installation, maintenance, training, service hotline, all of which is intangible, that brings this lump alive and makes it of use, in that it can fulfill the desired function, to help:

- Run the business accounts,
- Process management information,
- Enable the business to communicate, internally and externally,
- Design the firm's products or even, in the case of a small office/home office (SOHO) entertain the youngsters in the family.

Service: ADDING VALUE to the product

Service can also be used purely to add value, to either another service or to a good, or an existing combination of the two. The difference between the example of the PC as given above, and the aspect we now discuss, is that in the case of the PC the good is not a product without the services mentioned, whereas in the case (illustrated below), the 'product' could stand on its own without the (additional) service or services, the utility provided would be sufficient to address the majority of the customer's needs.

We address a very useful way of examining this issue in Chapter 7 when we consider the 'Levitt Construct'.

Some immediate examples of this are:

- a ready made suit vs. the bespoke tailor,
- a general construction company vs. a design build company,
- 'off the peg' open courses vs. client specific courses tailored by a professional institute's training business.

The tailor's normal fitting service can be augmented by:

- keeping a tailor's dummy sized to a regular customer, thus saving a considerable number of fittings, perhaps reducing these to just the final one.
- visiting the client at either their home, or place of work to conduct these fittings. This is a service that has been the norm for military tailors dealing with their officer clients, and which is now being extended to busy senior executives in the City. In this latter case the attraction for the client is not just convenience, the extra prestige of having one's tailor conduct a fitting whilst conducting routine business is proving a real client benefit.

The design, build, construction company reduces the need to deal with other suppliers; it effectively becomes 'a one-stop shop' when the client requires a new building.

The professional institute, like any training organization will provide a 'training needs analysis' service for its in-company work (as opposed to its public courses), but in addition could provide a follow-up 'hand-holding' service whereby the client is assisted in applying the skill acquired, and followed up on a regular basis afterwards to ensure that these skills do not atrophy, nor are bad habits acquired.

It is useful to categorize these additional value-added services under two headings:

1. **those for which the customer can be charged.**

   This does not have to be the case, indeed in the author's consultancy experience these are not infrequently ***given away***[17], and

2. **those, which although they may not attract a fee, are strategically the most important.**

It is also useful to know when, within the process of relationship building (part of the 'sales process'), it is best to use these additions.

Explanation with examples are provided after each of the lists below:

CHARGEABLE ADDITIONAL SERVICES
(i.e. customer can be charged for them)

THE SERVICE	when in the sales process BEFORE	DURING	AFTER
TRAINING	✓	✓	✓
HOTLINE		✓	✓
ANALYSIS	✓	✓	
CONSULTANCY	✓		
AUDIT	✓		
FUNDING	✓		
STOCK MANAGEMENT		✓	✓
INSURANCE			✓
MAINTENANCE			✓
UPGRADE			✓
WARRANTY			✓

TRAINING – is perhaps the most potent of these services: it provides ample opportunity to build and maintain relationships with many members of the DMU, provides long-term contacts and ensures that the service marketer keeps in touch with events within the clients' firm.

HOTLINE – enabling a customer to gain access to advice and help on demand. An aspect that has become a major feature in the IT industry, formerly a competitive edge, now very much a necessity (see Chapters 5).

ANALYSIS – undertaken to discover how the customer is currently performing in the job, and to provide the basis on which suggestions for improvement can be made. Perhaps one of which is to employ your 'product'.

CONSULTANCY – helping the customer improve one or more aspects of their business, though not necessarily via the use of your product. As with 'Training' above, an ideal way to maintain long-term contact in order to husband the relationship.

AUDIT – the intelligent combination of the last two. A favorite method used by the author when a Divisional Manager of an international tyre manufacturer:

> *'By prior arrangement with the proprietors, our teams would visit the vehicle parks of road transport companies, (lorry and bus), survey their tyres and analyze how well their use was managed. The fruit of this was the presentation of a report demonstrating how this aspect of the firm's business could be improved so as to better comply with motor industry legislation, and more importantly to reduce costs.*
>
> *Our recommendations would often include a commendation of a stock management system, (see below). As a result, even though our tyres were fairly run-of-the-mill, compared with Michelin, we obtained the lion's share of the UK bus tyre market, and a very healthy share of the tyre business of the UK lorry fleets.'*

STOCK MANAGEMENT – helping the customer obtain efficiencies via lower inventory carrying costs sometimes associated with 'just in time' deliveries. Tire companies do this with large fleet users. Form printers do this with customers who have a high consumption of pre-printed stationery such as invoices, statements and cheques.

The author has recently learnt of a major wine importer, whose main TG is the up-market (expensive) restaurants of London and the Home Counties. This 'service product' reduces price sensitivity to their wines and is a way to lock-in these customers to the one supplier[18].

FUNDING – a major factor in many businesses is to help the customer buy your product. Estate agents help customers to find mortgages, the defense and the international construction industries see it as a vital part of their know-how, to be able to help their clients raise loans and grants so as to make the required purchases.

INSURANCE – MAINTENANCE – UPGRADE – WARRANTY – the reader will be very familiar with how these are used to husband relationships with customers. If examples are required, consider the IT industry where these facets are now *sinequanon*.

MOST STRATEGICALLY IMPORTANT
(i.e. no fee charged but builds the relationships)

	when in the sales process		
THE SERVICE	BEFORE	DURING	AFTER
DEMONSTRATION	✓		
CASE STUDY	✓		
APPLICATIONS KNOW-HOW	✓		
TESTING		✓	✓
PROCESS REPORTS		✓	
SPEED OF REACTION	✓		
TREND ANALYSIS			✓
REMINDERS			✓
NEW IDEAS			✓
NEW PRODUCTS			✓
GUARANTEED BUY-BACK	✓		✓

DEMONSTRATION – show the prospect what your firm can do for them, sometimes linked to 'reference sites'. It is where a customer has agreed to allow your firm to either bring other potential customers to see your product[19] in action, and/or to refer your potential customers to see it for themselves.

A trick frequently missed is to provide an incentive for the 'reference site' to pass on the leads thereby obtained.

CASE STUDY – using the same principle as above, let the prospect know how your product can be applied, but in this case it is usually all on paper. But nowadays it could so easily be on DVD.

APPLICATIONS KNOW-HOW – helping the customer to apply your product in their specific, perhaps unique circumstances.

TESTING – making sure that the product is being used to its full advantage, and or that it has been installed or constructed (by the customer, or an independent installer) according to specification. A leading UK producer of self-assembly airplanes supplies a test pilot to check out the finished airplane before the customer incurs the cost of a government inspector's examination of the aircraft for its airworthiness certificate.

PROGRESS REPORTS – keeping the customer informed of progress on a long job, such as during a major market research study. In this case, as in many others, the benefit can be that it enables the customer to steer the project in the light of what has been encountered so far, thus adding to the richness and utility of the work being done.

SPEED OF REACTION – as will be seen in Chapter 4, a key issue in any business is the ability to compete in time (CIT). How quickly a firm can respond to a customer's needs can often be the deciding factor. A financial institution that takes too long to process an application for say a mortgage, insurance, or a pension could well be left out in the cold. A major study of this issue by the Boston Consulting Group has shown that in such processes, a solid 17 minutes of work on that application is all that is often necessary, and yet it was then not unusual for the organization to take upward of 12 days to get back to the customer with a firm offer (often the cause of this is poor resource management – see Chapter 9).

TREND ANALYSIS – keeping the customer informed as to what is happening in their industry as far as your product is concerned. A major photo-processing laboratory, selling color processing through major retail chains conducts regular market research into the photographic habits of the UK population. This information is passed on to the retail chains as part of the photo-lab's total product, helping to keep their clients ahead of other retailers in this market.

REMINDERS – the author's dentist, as do many others, regularly sends him reminders of when the next visit is due. In addition, the dentist's receptionist calls the night prior to an appointment to remind the client of tomorrow's appointment. This is a practice that many (but not nearly enough) firms emulate, from motor servicing, local health centers, restaurants, insurance etc.

NEW IDEAS – this is a frequent and key practice of advertising agencies. They take on the role of their customers' opportunity spotting department. Often people within the client's firm will have spotted those opportunities already but will have learned through bitter experience that *'a prophet is rarely,* *if ever, recognized in their own country'*, whereas an outsider has no such inhibition.

(The irony is that the first place where the astute outsider will usually fish for these 'new' ideas is inside the firm.)

It was ever so, when, in the late 15th century the merchants of Bristol, on receipt of the news of the discoveries of Christopher Columbus, hired the Cabot family to discover a bit of the New World for themselves. The first place that John and Sebastian Cabot visited was the 'Welsh Back' quays in Bristol's dockland. It was here that the long distance fishermen landed their salt cod caught on the distant Grand Banks. These fishermen told their fellow seaman where to look; they had long since given up on the merchants of Bristol.

NEW PRODUCTS – as above, in principle.

GUARANTEED BUY-BACK – helping the customer, consumer or commercial, to manage their costs more effectively by guaranteeing to buy back the good at a guaranteed price. This is fast becoming a favorite feature in the motor industry, specifically with the fleet market, but now also extending to new car sales to individuals.

It is usual for the vendor to insist that the distributor's facilities maintain the vehicle as part of the conditions of the guarantee, thus increasing their service business.

The re-purchased car now passes into the second-hand market under the control of the manufacturer, enabling them to influence that market more effectively than ever before.

Motor manufacturers are also facilitating the end of life buy-back by increasingly building their vehicles of re-usable parts and recyclable materials, thus additionally enhancing their credentials for having a care for the environment.

Exercise

Consider both the Chargeable Additional Services and Most Strategically Important lists. The questions are:

1. Which of these approaches is the most suitable for your type of business?
2. Why one and not the other? Of the list that is the most suitable consider:
   i. Are there some items on this list you are not doing – and should be doing? If so
   ii. Think how best you can start implementing this missed opportunity and how you are going to introduce it to your clients.

References

14 *See Chapter 7 – Making the Service Tangible.*

15 *See Chapter 7 re Making the Service Tangible for the anecdote re the encounter with a grimy barrister.*

16 *The cost of their upkeep in the face of aggressive growth of 'tele-banking' etc., is now causing 'The Banks' in particular to close these branches wholesale. Soon they will be subsumed into the former service category, i.e. where there will be few naturally occurring tangibles and therefore something physical will have to be deliberately supplied.*

17 *With the unfortunate result that the client takes them for granted, and values them very little, because that is what they cost.*

18 *The benefit for the customer restaurant is relatively little capital tied up in the wine cellar and positive cash flow, the restaurant only pays when the wine has been sold.*

FOUR

Competing in time (CIT)

FOUR

Competing in time (CIT)

Introduction

"The race does not always go to the swift, but that's the way to bet!!..."

Anon

This chapter examines the five 'flavours of time' and the way it affects the marketing of service businesses.

It enjoys a chapter all to itself because of its often little recognized importance to the customers' perception of the total service product.

Time is, after all, the only means whereby a service can be objectively measured.

Time – the only objective measure

As has already been mentioned, the issue of time can be a threat to a service business because a service is 'perishable', it has no shelf life. At its heart, a service consists of no more than the use of a resource over time. For example:

- a plane seat until we reach New York,
- a consultant day,
- a computer facility by the minute, e.g. 30 minutes in an internet cafe accessing emails.

'Time' is utterly non-renewable, thus unsold 'past' resource-time has gone forever, the firm may only sell future resource time.

However, time can also be a source of great opportunity to the creative service Marketer, so much so that two senior partners, of the Boston Consulting Group (George Stalk Jnr and Tom Houte), have produced a seminal book on this topic *"Competing Against Time"*.

Time is a powerful segmentation variable for the service sector, indeed, as already indicated it is the only 'objective' dimension on which the customer can gauge quality.

The five flavours of time

Time comes in five 'flavours' (for want of a better description) which are:

1. **Punctuality**
2. **Duration**
3. **Availability**
4. **Speed of response and**
5. **Speed of innovation**

We examine each in turn.

Punctuality

As seen in Chapter 3 when people are asked "What is the important factor used to judge a service?", 'reliability', 'responsiveness' and 'assurances' come top of the list of 35 factors. Between them these accounted for 75% of the respondents questioned. Further research to investigate what is actually meant by these responses reveals that time keeping (punctuality) is **THE** underlying anxiety.

Does the service supplier keep to the times announced/agreed?

- Will the airline fly to the published schedule so that a passenger can be reasonably assured of making that connection and thus also making that meeting in Milan?
- Will the consultant's report be available for the client to build its findings into next year's business plan?
- Will my local doctor deal with me within ten minutes of the appointment time or will I be kept waiting (without a word of explanation) all morning?

And, what does happen when schedules slip?

- Are customers kept informed promptly – or do they have to complain before being put in the picture?

Also, what assurances, guarantees and compensation does the customer get when the service provider fails to be punctual.

The golden rules for service punctuality are:

1. Never plan or publish a schedule that has too little 'slack', i.e. margin to absorb delays outside your control.
2. If possible, promulgate events not as a discrete point in time, but as occurring within a bracket (e.g. 15 minutes).
3. Back-up assurances/guarantees with compensation for the customer, e.g. penalty clauses, discount vouchers, etc., if not delivered within 30 minutes.

Domino's Pizzas promised at first to deliver the order within 30 minutes of receiving it, or the customer gets the pizza free. They then progressed to 30 minutes or they would knock $3.00 off the price. *(Eventually, because of the number of accidents caused to and fro by speedy pizza deliveries – the company in the USA were forced to abandon this promise).*

The interesting thing is that when they initially set up the company, Domino's researched the market during which they discovered that the mode (average) delivery time was 26 minutes – their promotion promised to be below average (which not too many customers realized). But the bold claim supported by assurances and compensation if they were in default, helped the company to grow from zero to over 5,000 outlets by the time they could no longer use this promise.

And if things do go wrong, and if the firm wishes to retain its credibility, the iron law– is to get back to the customer with a firm offer for compensation within 24 hours if possible but always within the first 48 hours.

Duration

This is to do with how long the performance of the service lasts. Frequently service marketers will use this duration to calculate their costs, and perhaps even charge for the service as a function of the time consumed (e.g. the consultant by the hour, the trainer by the day, the telephone by the call unit etc.). It will depend on the situation as to whether the customer perceives value as a function of the time taken to perform the service and whether this is a direct or inverse function. There are occasions (e.g. dentists) where the quicker a certain part of the service is performed, the better the customer likes it, and others (e.g. aroma therapy massage) where the longer it takes, the greater the perception of value by the customer.

If the service marketers' business corresponds to the first case (dentist), then attention is paid to minimizing the 'perceived' amount of time in which the customer experiences discomfort and to maximizing the social interaction afterwards.

The perception issue is critical, as illustrated by the strategy adopted by Disney for those queuing for a ride (the Americans call this a 'line-out'). The place where guests are asked to queue is marked out, and working back from the start of the queue the lineout is marked with timings (ten minutes – 20 minutes – 30 minutes etc.). This indicates how long the guest can expect to wait from this spot before they get to the front of the queue. These indications always over-estimate how long the queue will take (i.e. it under promises). For example at the point where experience shows it will take (say) 15 minutes to reach the ride, the indicator will show an expected wait of 20 minutes, thus when the guest arrives at the front it will be a shorter wait than expected (i.e. they have over delivered).

If the second situation applies, i.e. the longer the duration the greater the perceived value, then especially in slack times, (see The resource dilemma, Chapter 9) the service marketer should aim to deliver a little more than expected. Never appear to be in a rush to conclude the service delivery, even in busy times. An example of this is the consultant or trainer who is prepared to stay on after the session to answer queries and discuss implications with their clients.

Availability

A major source of competitive advantage, for which in many markets customers will pay handsomely, is to be able to access the service when it's convenient to them.

Any firm with an international dimension to its service must provide its customers with access to the right help and advice etc. whenever the customer may require it. This means 24 hours per day, because international business never sleeps. The customer in Hong Kong say, or the customer in Chile, will require contact when convenient to them, i.e. during their working day, which means out of hours in Europe.

If the reader has any doubts about time as a differentiator, consider the success of 'First Direct' the telephone-banking arm of the Midland Bank. Whilst they were not the first telephone banking operation in the UK (that distinction belongs to the Giro Bank), First Direct was the first that was available 24 hours a day, every day of the year.

Within two years of its start-up, First Direct was taking considerable numbers of its customers from some of the most prestigious private banks in the UK.

Research conducted by some of these private banks to investigate this attrition, showed that the major reason for defection was the customer convenience of being able to bank whenever they wanted, and wherever in the world they found themselves at that time.

The fact that customers will pay a great deal for the convenience of accessing the service when they want, is illustrated by the large commissions, and the wide 'spreads' charged by Bureau de Change in the tourist areas of big cities such as London, Paris, Kuala Lumpur and New York.

These businesses have segmented their market well. Their target group is those who have not been able to get to a bank or building society when these facilities were open, either because they forgot, or they had not had the opportunity. In these circumstances, if the tourist wishes to convert their currency they have only the alternatives of their hotel or at the Bureau de Change, and neither is loathe to charge for the convenience.

Speed of response

HOW QUICKLY DOES YOUR FIRM GET BACK TO THE CUSTOMER?

How long does it take your business to process an item of administration such as a proposal, an insurance policy, holiday itinerary report of findings?

The speed with which this is done can provide the two major benefits of:

- competitive advantage and
- cost reduction.

COMPETITIVE ADVANTAGE derives from either the added convenience thus provided to the customer (i.e. they are not kept waiting) and/or from getting to the customer first.

To gain this advantage the service marketer should concentrate on eliminating delay from the systems which deliver the key part of the service. In the vast majority of cases this is intimately related to the capacity of these systems, and how they are organized. (We examine this under The resource dilemma in Chapter 9.)

In far too many cases the administrative process involves a disproportionate amount of time waiting for the next action to be taken, compared to the very small amount of time in which value is actually being added. *Competing Against Time* (George Stalk Jnr and Tom Houte) cites the '5% to 0.5% Rule'. The B.C.G. research (and this author's experience) suggests that at best, value has only added some 5% of the total time that the process takes. At worst this can be as little as only half of one per cent of the time. Which means to say that for at least 95% of the time nothing is happening, it's either metaphorically or actually sitting in someone's in-tray waiting.

Competing Against Time quotes the case of an insurance company where the production of an insurance proposal to a customer normally takes (i.e. the 'mode') some 20 days from when the client provided his/her details, to when the client receives the proposal. During these 20 days value was being added (i.e. someone was working on it) for a total of only 17 minutes.

This is said to be one of the greatest 'good news – bad news' stories.

GOOD NEWS in that if the service marketer were to just start looking at the situation it can only get better, it shouldn't take much to at least halve the time taken.

BAD NEWS in that if the firm does not address this issue first, it will 'get its hide nailed to the wall' by its competition.

This has already happened in the financial services sector with the rise of the 'Directs' (Direct Line, First Direct, Virgin Direct et al). Their speed of process has benefited greatly from the necessary incorporation of computer-based administration which provides 'on-line' quotation and processing facilities.

But competing in time has also proved to be an advantage elsewhere. A major provider of components to the aero-engine business has gained an international market share for its high technology flexible hoses, as used in the fuel systems of the modern passenger jet, by guaranteeing that wherever the airplane is in the world, they will supply the necessary replacement part within 24 hours of receiving notification.

Similarly, a German specialist boot maker obtained the exclusive contract to supply the Household Cavalry[20] with its riding boots, thus ending several hundred years of business for the former UK supplier. The new firm's tender was not the cheapest by far (so we are informed) but they did undertake to eliminate the need to carry stocks of the expensive boots worn on ceremonial occasions. If a replacement is required, even of only one boot, they undertake to supply that item to the Cavalry Unit within 24 hours, wherever that unit happens to be in the world.

In both of the above cases, the facility offered exploits the phenomena that:

- The more customers for whom stock is held centrally, the lower the ratio of stock required per customer,
- The probabilities of stock items being required can be calculated with reliability, and
- Strategically located warehouses (global couriers like UPS, DHL and Fed Ex) plus modern computer-based stock control and ordering, enable rapid response with lowest cost.

COST REDUCTIONS that are obtained via shortening the time taken to perform a given administrative process derive from a combination of sources. However, the plain fact of the matter is that it is improbable that a task taking 17 minutes can cost as much as the same tasks taking 20 days.

Speed of innovation

Getting a technology to market before the competition can be of tremendous benefit particularly, and most reliably, in the short-term[21]. In the right sort of marketplace this ability provides a profitable window of opportunity during which time the service marketer has a monopoly on the innovation and can charge for it.

GESTATION – The period of time from concept to launch. As in the human life cycle, this period, together with the next two, 'Introduction' and 'Growth', requires an enormous amount of investment.

The cost of this investment is compounded by the failure rate experienced. The ratio is exceedingly high between the number of those service products that are introduced only to fall by the wayside, compared to the number that attain the goals originally set for them.

Marketers' skills at new product development (NPD) are improving. In the early 1960s the rate was circa 58:1, (i.e. one success for every 58 ideas) it is now said to be circa 16:1. Even so this is still a very expensive failure rate and there are other ways of doing things.

A major cause of failure (and consequent loss) with new service products is caused by the service marketer often not being in control of the gestation period.

A tenet of NPD is that to overspend an NPD budget by 50% will shave some 4% off the eventual profit of the project. However, if the project is as little as six months late, profits will take a minimum of a 23% hit, (always assuming that the product does not miss its window of opportunity altogether.)[22]

The ease with which the gestation period is controlled depends on the extent to which the extra benefits to be provided via the innovation of the new service product are related (or are not related) to the development of any technology[23].

Technology: Pull versus push

It could perhaps be argued that some service products are 'technology neutral', that is to say, there is no significant benefit provided via a technological innovation even indirectly. However, it is difficult to think of any. The author has recently witnessed a local landscape gardener surveying a new job via the use of what can only be described as a 'laser range finder', and also the collection and dispatch of soil samples for sophisticated mineral analysis.

Technology pull

This is where a demonstrated gap in the market exists, (there is a clear need for specific new benefits) but the technology has yet to be developed to fill that gap.

For example, the perceived gap in the market for electronic shopping said to be provided by the internet (perhaps like the 'Smart Card' of more benefit to the retailers than their public) which is 'pulling' the encryption aspects of Electronic Data Interchange (EDI) to develop the technology necessary for the secure communication of customers' credit card/charge card details (et al). ***OR***

Technology push

If the technology exists, and the NPD emphasis is on evolving ways (perhaps new ways) whereby this technology can be applied to advantage, then we term this 'Technology Push'. Paraphrased as – "We have the answer, now, what's the problem?" The current rush, for example, to find ways of using the internet to make a profit, it must be useful for something other than pornography, but what?

Technology pull: an example

In 1946, there was an obvious gap in the market for more comfortable, quicker ways to cross the Atlantic by air. Travel then involved four stages with planes flying much lower than today for much of the journey which resulted in uncomfortable flights. The flight times of each four stages could be as much as 15 hours upward.

That year The Bristol Aeroplane Company conceived of Concord (then spelt the English way), De'Haviland of St. Albans conceived of the Comet – which flew first, and this stimulated Boeing to adapt the B52 bomber into the very successful Boeing 707. For both Concord and the Comet, the gestation gap (from conception to consumption) was the killer (the brilliance of Boeing will be revisited at the end of this chapter).

The De'Haviland Comet was first built with rectangular, sharp cornered windows. As a result, previously un-encountered stress fractures caused several crashes, much loss of life, and an unacceptable reputation for the traveling public.

Concorde (now spelt the French way), did not carry its first fare paying passengers until 1977 (a 30 year gestation), by which time the market had moved away from the idea of mass supersonic travel when they discovered the unacceptability of:

- regular sonic booms over habitations,
- high altitude pollution from the nitrous oxide [NOX] of its original engine configuration, and
- acute jet lag (unknown in 1946).

So, although it appears commonsense to develop a service product in response to an identified 'gap in the market', the service marketer needs to gain a clear idea of the extent to which specific technologies will have to be developed, and the time taken in order to make the vision a reality.

Technology push: an example

In the late 1960s British Telecom engineers, stimulated by the need to find ways of loading the large amounts of spare exchange capacity in the UK, conceived of 'Prestel', which enabled people to use the telephone infrastructure to communicate visually (in a manner that is now called 'interactive'). A marvel of technology, Prestel had a wide range of uses, from examining what was happening on the Stock Exchange to electronic shopping, booking airline tickets and obtaining the weather reports – all in full color, but it never caught on.

In France, the government conceived the idea of using the telephone infrastructure to communicate visually as a unique way of forcing the pace of the diffusion of technological literacy amongst their public. In consequence all telephone directories were withdrawn, and this facility was then made available on Minitel, the French equivalent of Prestel. It was an inferior technology and functionality was in black and white only, but the idea was a success.

But consider the internet; is this not but a more glorious, less disciplined Prestel but by another name?

In the late 70s only 180,000 homes and offices had a Prestel terminal. In the early 2000s the internet already had an average of c.40% penetration of all homes in developed countries.

In the very early 1970s, a group of what would now be called 'nerds', became fascinated by the idea of building and programming their own home 'micro' computers. Two of these 'nerds' called Steve (Wozniak and Jobs respectively) eventually had the ridiculous idea that people like you and I would want one of these on our desks. Thus did Apple beget the microcomputer which was eventually to be adopted by IBM and renamed the Personal Computer, and because IBM is American, henceforth to be known worldwide by its initials as the 'PC'.

For neither the PC, Prestel or for the internet was there ever a gap in the market. No market research company would ever have been able to prove any demand for such a thing, yet look at them now!

Thus the service marketer will have to tolerate and encourage those people in their teams who believe in an idea for a new service product, sometimes just because it can be done, even in the face of apparently little demand. If the reader should want any further confirmation of the benefits of self-confidence, consider Baron Bic and his disposable razors, but that product is of course a 'good', and therefore perhaps we in services should ignore it, we are different after all.

One particular example of how speedy innovation can prove profitable in the service sector was the building of the Boeing 777.

The Boeing 777 airplane took five years from conception to the first fare-paying passenger flying on it. It is a super plane to fly in from the passenger's point of view; Cabin Class on today's Boeing 777 is more luxurious than was First Class on the 707. Boeing had this market to themselves and it took several more years before the Airbus equivalent was in service. In the meantime, airlines compete for delivery of their 777s because each day that their passengers have to fly on older aircraft puts them at a disadvantage relative to airlines where the passengers can enjoy the 777.

Contrast this situation with Concorde, a wonderful piece of engineering, but from conception to consumption took some 30 years, with the result that it missed its market and only 17 commercial planes were ever built instead of the 200-300 originally envisaged (or even the one hundred options to buy that were taken out by airlines just after the maiden flight in 1968).

On a different scale, Tom Peters cites Cable News Network[24] as another example. Their ability to compress the development process of news delivery means that they are often (too often for the other broadcasters) able to run first with breaking news, wherever the occasion may occur in the world. The result has been phenomenal growth and incorporation into one of the world's largest news and information providing conglomerates[25].

Exercise

1. Via consultation with a few customers who you feel are representative of the general body of your customer base – get them to tell you how your business could improve in terms of the 'Flavors of Time' we have discussed so far – and
2. If you were to take action on these findings, work out what changes you would have to make to implement the time related improvements your customers have recommended.
3. Cost out these changes and then see if there will be a monetary advantage – if so
4. Plan the implementation of the changes recommended.

References

19 *Good and/or Service 'Product'.*

20 *Part of the ceremonial bodyguard of the British monarch.*

21 *We discuss the fact that in the service sector being first may not be as attractive as is supposed to be, long or short term.*

22 *Dr. William E. Coyne, Senior Vice President, Research and Development of 3M*

23 *("i.e. the application of scientific understanding to commerce", which takes in much more than IT, even though that is what most frequently springs to mind whenever the term Technology is used).*

24 *"Get Fast or Go Broke" – Tom Peter's Video*

25 *Telecommunications International [TCI] itself now merged with Time Warner.*

FIVE

The service product and its positioning

FIVE

The service product and its positioning

Introduction

"The ability to learn faster than the competition, and act more swiftly may, in the future, be our only sustainable competitive advantage."

Dr. Arie de Geus – Royal Dutch Shell

This chapter considers the use of the Levitt Construct as a tool with which to examine those aspects of the service product that are important to, and valued by, the customer.

It illustrates this via the way that airlines have differentiated themselves, and proceeds to examine how this is applies to two other service businesses, the health care sector, and taxi firms.

This then enables the marketer to position a service product with a differential advantage over the offerings of the competitors. Here we introduce the 'Product Wheel' tool to assist positioning decision making.

This section concludes with a discussion of the ways to handle the major downside of a service, you will be copied if successful, and how the service marketer handles that fact.

Positioning the service product

The need

Primarily the need is to position the service product in the market so that in the perception of the customer, there are no acceptable alternatives. Done well, this will mean that the product has a Competitive Differential Advantage (CDA) over the rest of the market, especially for the designated target group of customers (as we will see, the two are indivisible, the product from its market or vice versa).

The service marketer uses positioning to differentiate their product offering particularly in the perception of the customers.

Repositioning is required especially when the product is approaching that part of its Product Life Cycle concept (PLC) where growth is starting to tail off, and the far sighted members of the team can already discern the outline of future replacement.

Introducing the 'Levitt Construct Tool'

Theodore Levitt, a Professor of Marketing at Harvard (aren't they all, but his pedigree is hard to beat) is the Father of the 'Product Life Cycle' concept and has suggested the following tool[26], which this author has taken further, specifically applying it to the service product. The tool provides service marketers with a unique way of viewing their products and identifying those areas where effort to improve its competitive advantage will have the greatest payback.

The structure of the tool is normally communicated via the use of the following diagram:

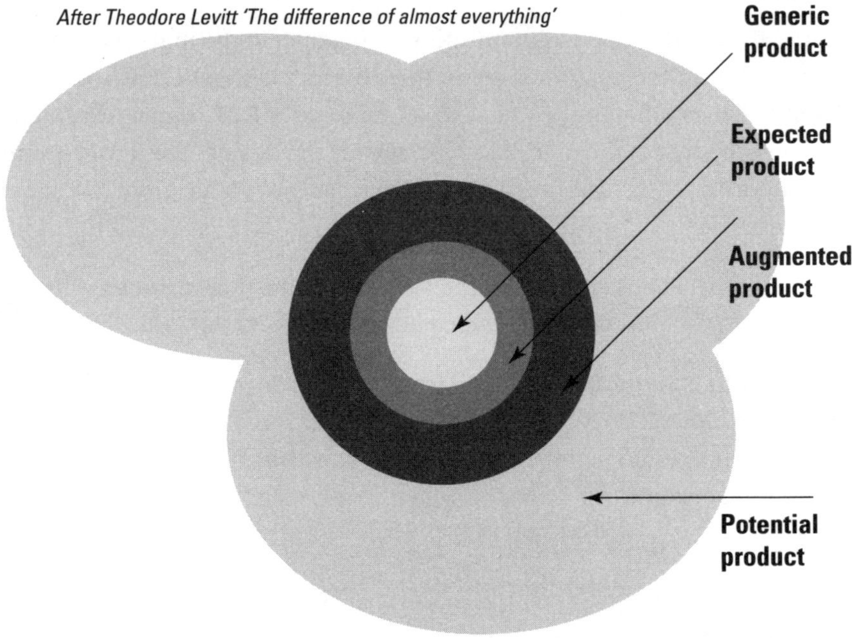

5.1: THE TOTAL SERVICE PRODUCT CONCEPT

In this construct, the service product is said to consist of three overlaying strata, each completely surrounding the one below. These layers are arranged like the layers of a fruit, say a peach, first the kernel (*GENERIC*), within the stone's shell (*EXPECTED*), all covered by the flesh of the fruit (*AUGMENTED*).

The whole thing is within an aura of what it could be, (*POTENTIAL*). **This part having no boundaries other than our own imagination.**

We proceed to examine each layer in turn using the airline business to illustrate:

The generic product

The paradox really is that from the service operations/delivery point of view this is the most important part of the product, however, as long as the team gets it right, it has very little impact on the customer. The 'generic product' represents the 'mission-critical' part of the business operations, i.e. the vast majority of the skills, effort and cost that goes into providing a given service.

Some commentators believe that from 70% upward of our skills, effort and cost are spent on this part of the product, BUT that it contributes less than 5% of the reasons why customers may choose us over the competition.

In the case of an airline business, the 'generic' would include:

- maintaining the airframe, engines, electronics, and running gear of the planes,
- all the operations required to turn the planes round at the end of each flight. Such as cleaning inside and out, emptying the tanks that must be emptied, filling those that must be full at take off, loading passengers' luggage and consumables like the in-flight meals, checking the safety of tyres and the security of the plane from terrorist attack etc. etc.
- ticketing, flight reservations administration, check-in procedures etc.
- training, initial and continuous, from the flight deck crew, to the cabin crew to the ground staff, etc., and
- the basic administration of the business itself, (no mean task but one most airlines do very well).

The list goes on. However, it will be noticed that most of the above is 'out of sight and out of mind' for the traveling public – until things go wrong.

If things go well, then the typical traveler takes this part for granted. They do not feel able to judge, even though their lives depend on the airline doing it perfectly (99.9% error free is not acceptable, it is the equivalent of one Jumbo crash each week at either Heathrow or Chicago).

Few passengers have ever been seen checking the airplane's tyres for bald patches before getting aboard.

BUT it only takes a slight hitch in the wrong place for that trust to evaporate. A maxim of the President of 'Pan American', a famous international airline in the early 1960s, still applies:

"When a customer pulls down their seat table to discover loose screws and a coffee stain growing mould from several flights ago, they can be excused for believing that this is the same level of attention we pay to the engines."

Two lessons are to be drawn from this:

1. Any promotion which features a firm's ability in this part of the product will have little impact on the customer, they take for granted that the firm knows what it is doing, **as long as nothing** (that the customer can see) **goes wrong with this part of the product.**

And following on from this:

2. The service marketer must ensure that the delivery team knows how important it is to have regard for the little things that could alarm a customer, no matter how apparently trivial they may seem to be.

Expected product

Unlike the 'generic' the expected part of the product is understandable to the customer. It is used by them to evaluate the service providers' performance. However, the effect it has on their buying behavior is more re-active than pro-active. Customers treat this part of the product as a Hygiene Factor[27], in that customers regard this part of the product as the minimum acceptable standard performance for the industry. The ability to deliver this part of the service product is the basic qualification for being in the given service market.

All 'players' in this market will perform this part of their service in an acceptable way. Customers will not be attracted because of what is expected of them, but customers will be lost if perceived performance **does not meet** expectation.

In the case of an airline, the 'expected' part of the product will include:

- Baggage handling, efficient reservations, courteous check-in, in-flight meals, drinks, duty free, in-flight entertainment etc.

The customer can judge if:

- their baggage turns up on time in the right place,
- the food is hot (if it is supposed to be),
- adequate and timely drinks, entertainment, duty free service etc are or are not provided to the expected standard.

In addition to this for a customer to consider a particular candidate for an impending journey, each airline will be assessed along the lines of:

- Do they go to the intended destination:
  - Direct or will the customer have to change flights, if so how many times?
  - Is the airline's schedule convenient to the customer's intended schedule?
  - If the customer is a frequent flyer, does the airline belong to the same 'AirMiles' incentive scheme as the customer uses?

Service businesses that do not supply these 'expected' parts of the product will either require to have a price differential to justify (e.g. Ryan Air, when they started, for example, offered 'no frills flights' from Dublin to London for £46.00 return, vs. Aer Lingus £128 return) or no competition on that route. For example within the authors lifetime, BA on some Scottish routes where there was no competition, no breakfast was served. However, on other Scottish routes where BA **were** in competition, they provide all the 'expected product'.

There is another lesson here:

Baggage handling is most often done by the airport facilities, not by the airline themselves, but if the passenger to Majorca discovers that some items of their holiday baggage have gone on to Madrid, or even worse, to Moscow instead, it is the airline which gets the blame. They were the ones to whom the passenger entrusted their luggage at the check-in desk. The service business takes full responsibility for whatever is done for the customer in their name and within the service product. That is the way the customer perceives the issue, **their perception is all there is.**

The augmented product

This is the 'competitive edge', the 'motivational factor' (Hertzberg again) is what will bring new customers to the firm, stimulating them to leave suppli-
who they previously found to be satisfactory.

The irony is that this area of the service product may take less than 10% of the total time, effort, or cost that the firm puts into the product, but it can deliver more than 55% of the product's impact to the customer's decision to buy.

An example of this is Virgin Atlantic Airlines adopting and adapting the Swiss Air practice of a limousine service for businessmen visiting the City of London on a day trip. Virgin Atlantic applied the concept first on the flights between Heathrow and New York.

Within a catchment area of 100 miles or less to the UK airport (initially Gatwick) at one end, or to the relevant New York airport at the other, a limousine would collect the 'Business' and 'Upper Class' passengers from their home or office (as appropriate) and take them to the airport, at no extra charge. There would be a similar service at the destination. The same service took place on the return journey.

The idea was so successful that Virgin extended the service for its Business Class passengers on most other routes.

Whilst at the same time, nearly every airline that competed on the same routes were forced to adopt the Limousine Service for their Business and First Class passengers, or lose business to Virgin. An exception to this was British Airways Club Class where they tried to compete by offering Club facilities at the port of arrival as well as departure. These extras included the facility to freshen-up via a hot shower when the passenger de-planed, together with a secretarial service to help the Club passenger to arrange appointments et al. Over time this BA Arrival Lounge facility has been quietly dropped.

This way of 'augmenting' the Business Class service product proved so attractive to business travelers generally that all airlines in competition with Virgin et al for Business or Upper Class passengers now have to offer a similar limousine service.

Virgin Atlantic has gone on from this to be the first to provide each passenger (at first Business and Upper classes, now the whole plane) with their own in-flight visual entertainment with an LCD/TV screen fixed on the back of the seat in front. An advantage again quickly copied by all the major airlines.

At the time of writing, Virgin was developing the idea of in-flight gambling. Whilst BA Club was stressing that its business passengers can get a good nights sleep on seats that fold down into spacious flat beds – lets see who wins this one.

The potential product

This part of the service product is the reservoir of new ideas whereby the firm can gain the 'competitive edge'.

The extent of this reservoir is limited only by our own imagination. The service marketer should constantly be seeking new ideas to add to the list, and more importantly, they should be designing ways and means to implement these new ideas, BEFORE the firm is forced to do so by the competition, in other words **contingency planning**.

Exercise

Part 1: Improving a taxi business

Imagine the following scenario, you have just been left a small, profitable (though struggling) taxi business by a long forgotten relative. It consists of between five and ten cars and operates in the suburban fringes of a major city.

Rather than sell the business you are inclined to run it as a director installing some of your ideas to improve the poor quality of service that you have typically experienced whenever you have used a taxi elsewhere.

STAGE 1

Decompose the generic and the expected parts of a taxi product. Remember that the generic is something that the customer will probably not check or worry about until it goes wrong, for example, whether or how efficiently the engine has been serviced recently.

The expected is something that would be the minimum standard the customer may expect but would be used to illuminate unsuitable firms rather than a reason to buy; for example, the interior cleanliness of the taxi.

(You should be able to drum up at least ten ideas for each of the above in as many minutes.)

STAGE 2

Now brainstorm (preferably with one or more friends) what could be the augmented and expected CDA additions to the basic service that would attract customers to you and delight them when they use your taxi service.

(You should be able to drum up at least 20 ideas between you in less than half an hour brainstorming.)

STAGE 3

When you have completed Stage 1 and 2, check your ideas with the list shown at the end of this section. This was stimulated by Harvey McKay in his book *How to Swim with Sharks* and *not Lose your Shirt*.

Part 2: Improving your business

Conduct Stage 1 and 2 as above to clearly identify the generic and expected parts of your business and then brainstorm, with colleagues if possible, to create a bank of ideas as to where and how you can gain the competitive edge now (augmented) and in the future (potential).

Select those ideas that show promise and start to create a contingency plan as to how these would be put into effect when needed.

Don't classify them at this stage – await circumstances – then select those that are appropriate for implementation, then do so with alacrity.

The lessons from this are:

1. Some of the best sources (or stimulants) of ideas on how a service product can gain the edge, i.e. produce the 'augmented product' are:
   - from our customers – so – brainstorm them continually,
   - from our competitors, or others elsewhere in the service sector. (The key to success is not to adopt the idea unthinkingly, but to be able to adapt or, to translate the idea into the context of your marketplace.)

2. If your competition gets the 'edge' you would be negligent if you didn't at least copy them, and at best, regain the initiative with another way of 'augmenting' your service product. The competition should be allowed only the smallest window of opportunity to exploit their advantage, or the bottom-line of your firm **will suffer**, sooner rather than later.

And leading on from this:

3. The service marketer must have a constantly replenished reservoir of ways and means whereby they can regain the competitive edge, once they have been copied or surpassed by the competition – that's the job of the 'potential'.

Thus, some sources of ideas worth mentioning are:

- Customers
- Competitors' customers
- Potential customers
- Front line staff (i.e. the service deliverers),
- Other marketers' ideas *
- People who are totally naïve about the situation[28]

* To know what is important to the customer is prime. No idea should be implemented until it is absolutely clear that the customer will value it. (See Seriously seeking feedback, Chapter 13.)

However, the idea may be so new that there is no way that the customer can be expected to know whether they will find it of value. For example, in the summer of 1996 in Florida, Disney offered the parents of families visiting from Europe an educational experience, (learn a range of skills from Cordon Bleu cooking through to how to make an animated cartoon film and white water rafting etc.) whilst the children were engaged on the 'rides'.

If this is the case that it is so novel that customers have no previous experience to call on, then pilot the idea (as did Disney), the service marketer will find this policy is cheaper, quicker and more certain than market research on most occasions.

* Ideas that have potential in your market can be gleaned from almost any other market (never be too proud to copy, but remember, if you attribute the source, that's respectable, it's called scholarship, if you pass it off as your own, that's plagiarism).

However, the service marketer must take care not to merely transpose the idea, i.e. apply it in its original form. This way, there is a strong probability that, like a fish out of water, the initiative will suffocate and die. The skill is to 'translate' the idea into the context of the new market's circumstances so as to provide an acceptable probability of success. To do this the service marketer must know their own market intimately, i.e. where this new idea is to be used. (See Chapter 13, Seriously seeking feedback.)

How the service product should be presented

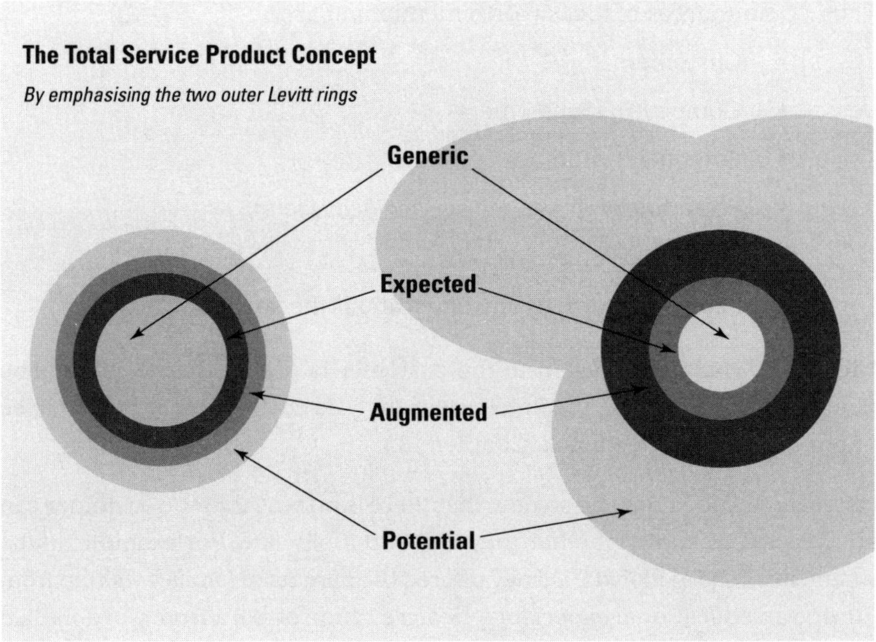

FIG 5.2: HOW THE SERVICE PRODUCT SHOULD BE PRESENTED

To the left of the above we see how too many service marketing businesses present themselves to their publics. The emphasis is on the 'generic', the core skills, that part which takes up most of their effort skill and cost, but which has little affect in persuading the prospect to switch to the service marketer's business away from their current suppliers.

The right hand part of the diagram exhibits how it should be, just enough 'generic' and 'expected' products to convince the customer or prospect that the firm knows its business. The main emphasis is on stressing the 'augmented' to provide the reasons why the prospect should consider switching.

In most service markets the firm should gain a reputation for always being innovative, for offering the customer something new and exciting over the offers of the competition, i.e. the 'potential' part of the service product.

The model applied elsewhere

In addition to the airline and Disney World examples mentioned above, the following will show that even at the other end of the scale of business size, and no matter where the firm is on the Service Spectrum, this construct can be a very useful positioning tool.

The health care industry

Various studies, both formal and informal, have been conducted to discover how local health care practices, health center clinics (partnerships of GPs with nurses etc. within the practice) and dental practices, both private and NHS, can make themselves more 'user friendly'. This is in preparation for the time when the 'practice' may wish to 'market' itself so as to attract more of the most profitable patients.

These studies invariably show that all the behind the scenes work of practice administration, organization, staff and partner training, keeping up to date in the disciplines, patient record keeping, etc. etc., in other words the 'generic product', is of little interest to the patients and their families (unless they should go wrong vis PanAm's President). These customers assume that the **professionals** in the practice know their job and will keep up to date.

The 'expected product'

This tends to be things like ease of parking, not too far to travel (the actual distance will vary depending on whether the practice is in a rural or urban area), 'reasonable' waiting time, ease of gaining an appointment, convenient surgery hours, can get to see your own doctor/dentist, sensitivity and tact from the reception staff. The list goes on, but the reader will have obtained the flavour.

The problem is:

- With a few notable exceptions, most of the above 'expected' part of the product is very uncertain, and often completely neglected.
- Health centres locate where they will provide indifferent parking, if at all (one the author knows makes patients 'pay and display' for the privilege of attending the surgery).
- Practices are frequently perceived as cavalier as to which doctor sees which patient. And the most frequent source of complaints is to do with the insensitivity of those on reception and the difficulties of obtaining an appointment when one is ill etc.
- However, many dentists seem by and large, to have 'cracked' most of this. It is not unusual for a dental practice to pay particular attention to making it easy for patients to gain appointments, and ensure sensitivity and consideration from the reception staff at all times.

The 'augmented product'

Dentists have led the way, not just in the UK, but apparently nearly all over the world. In a study carried out by a dental practice in Australia, the throughput of patients in a given year was divided into two matching samples, one the experimental sample and the other the control.

Those in the experimental sample were provided with a printout of the treatment that they had just received as they left the practice. Some two weeks later, together with a letter thanking them for their custom, the patients in this sample were sent a duplicate of the treatment form, a reminder of their medication (as appropriate), and a confirmation of the date of their next appointment. Two weeks prior to that next appointment a reminder was sent. And if the patient was working, the evening prior, they received a further confirmation by telephone to ensure that all was okay for the next day's appointment.

The control sample had none of these extras.

The result was that the patients in the experimental sample were **24 times** more likely to remain with that practice, than those in the control.

Apart from the very rare examples, GPs' health centers on the other hand seem still to be of a mind that patients should think themselves lucky to have any sort of health care available.

But it is changing, all be it slowly. A health centre in the West of England regularly conducts focus group discussions with its patients and their families to discover how it can bc more 'user-friendly'. The practice also provides a crèche, offers preventative medicine teach-ins for special groups of patients (e.g. young mums, those nearing retirement) provides local papers and non-machine tea or coffee whilst patients wait.

Not content with this, and to complement their special opening hours, in November 1995 a small kitchen was built within the practice to provide light refreshments such as breakfasts for the early risers, light lunches, and high teas for those who were being seen by the doctors in the late afternoon or evening.

It did not stop there, this practice came to national attention later that year (via articles in many broadsheets such as *The Times*[29]) when they were granted a wine license for evening meals served on the premises – now that's what the author calls a competitive advantage.

The point is that there is no service business that is too grand, humble or mundane to benefit from creative positioning using the Levitt Construct.

To do this successfully requires that the service marketing team should have open, curious and creative minds, and are skilled in the use of the creative thinking techniques of brainstorming, 'Synectics', 'De Bono's Six Thinking Hats', 'Tony Buzan's Mind Mapping', et al. This must be complemented by an emphatic determination and dedication to implement these ideas religiously and without fail.

So as to provide their creativity with the material and stimulus for the creative process they should also have access to the findings of the firm's CIS/MIS (See Chapter 13.)

The fundamentals of positioning a service product

The procedure

Positioning a service product starts as an inter-related, simultaneous comparison between the needs of a selected group of customers (the target group, or segment) and the strengths and weaknesses of the firms who are currently serving them (the competition).

SEGMENTING (TARGET CUSTOMERS)

Positioning should always start with a clear definition of the target group of customers (see Chapter 10). The moment a customer segment is defined, whether you know it or not, so is the competition. The probability that any potential customer is not already being served is almost zero.

COMPETITOR

An analysis of the competitor's strengths and weaknesses in relation to the service marketer's company should now take place. At this point it may be seen that the competition is too tough to be taken on with confidence, this may prompt a re-evaluation of how attractive it will be to pursue those target customers. Before proceeding further it may be better to seek another group of customers who are not so well defended. *Never engage in a conflict that you are not sure of winning.*

Part of the process of being sure that one can win against a given competitor is to identify what competitive advantage (the '**edge**') your service company can create for its offerings i.e. what will be the 'augmented' part of the service product. This requires that the service marketer understands the target group in depth.

TARGET CUSTOMERS

As we will see in Chapter 13, the service marketer must have an in depth understanding of the intended customer's needs, expectations, requirements and buying behavior. This is so as to identify the benefits (extra to what the competition offer) that will make the customer switch to his/her firm (and stay).

This will only happen if your offering more closely matches the customer's needs than does the offering from the competition. Below we set out a diagrammatic form of the process described above:

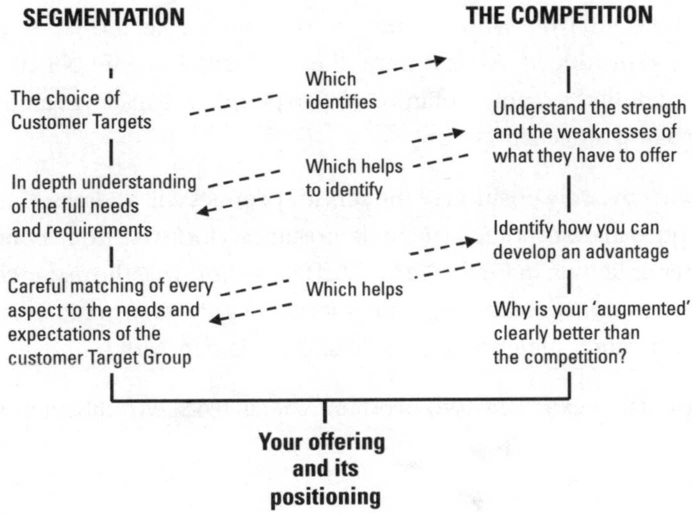

5.3: THE POSITIONING PROCESS

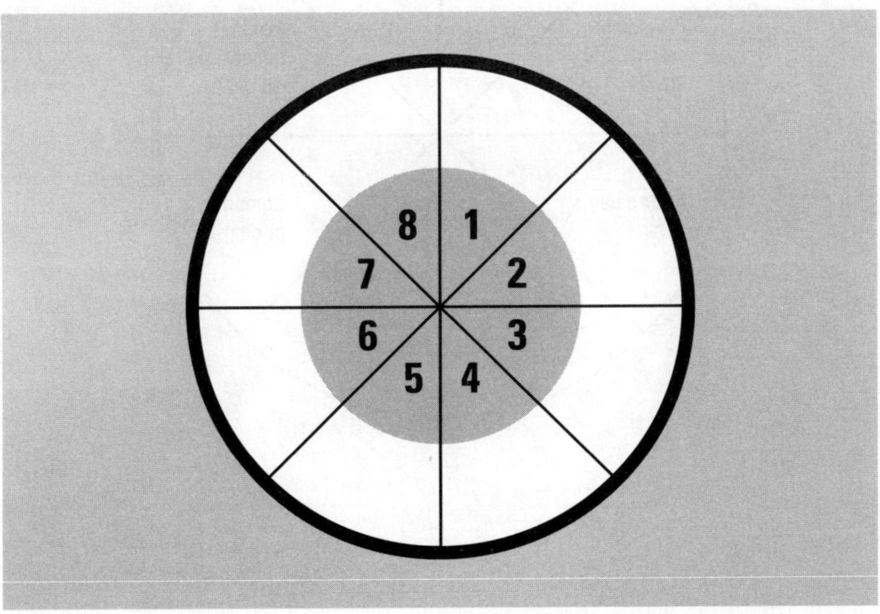

FIG 5.4: THE PRODUCT WHEEL, A USEFUL TOOL

This tool is borrowed from the armoury of the service sales teams.

The idea is to focus on eight (or less) factors that the customer uses to decide what, when, and from whom to buy in your market (i.e. the expected and the augmented products). A maximum of eight factors are set because of what is known about the amount of information people will use to evaluate choices when making a decision to buy[30].

To see what the new position of the service product will address, these factors are arranged in descending order of importance, clockwise from 'noon', around the center as shown in Figs 5.5 and 5.6. (*Please note that the distance between the factors is not constant, and nor is it necessarily very great, i.e. there may not be very much separating the first and the last factors.*)

We show, as an example, two product wheels from two different firms.

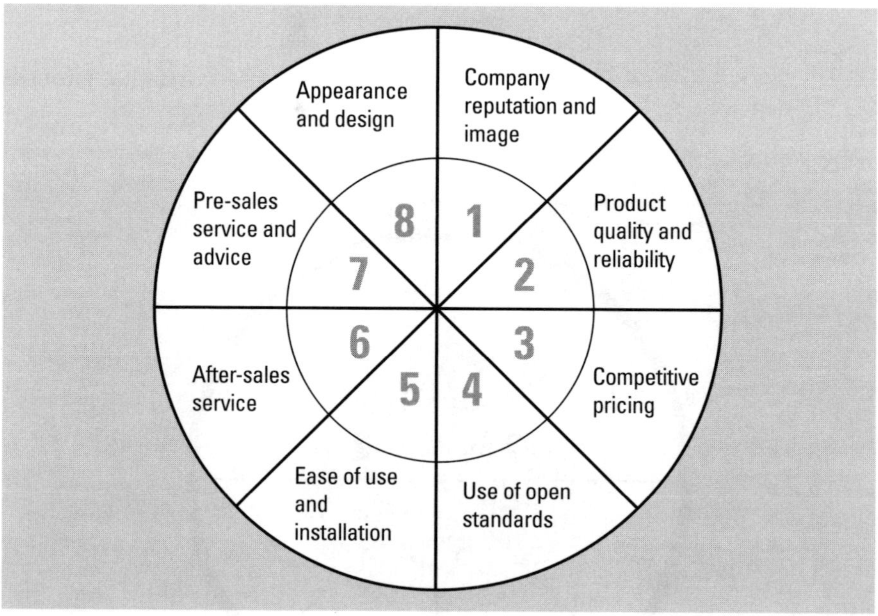

FIG 5.5

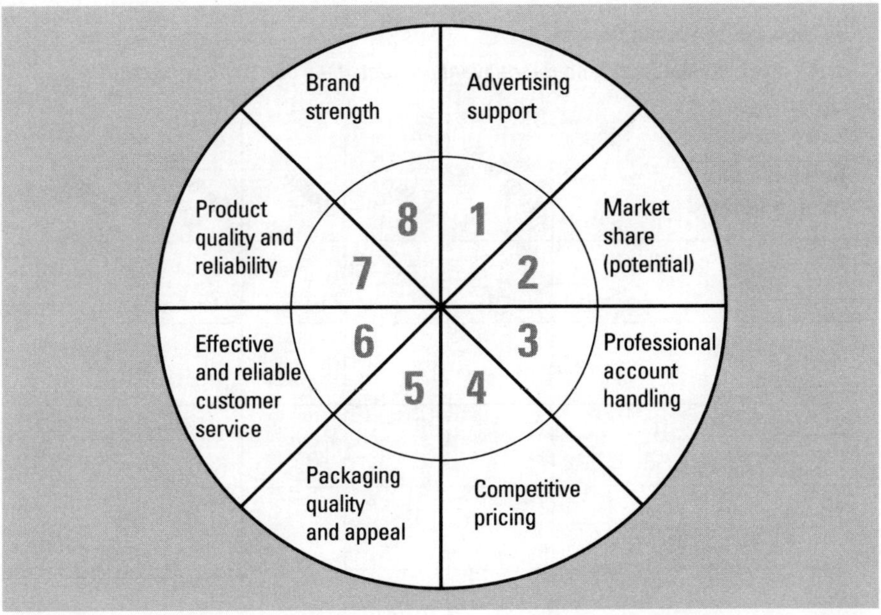

FIG 5.6

Fig 5.5 is from a company marketing computer hardware. The data resulted from a market research project examining how intermediaries evaluated dealing with one supplier versus another.

From this it can be seen that the service content, including the 'use of open standards', accounts for about half of the evaluative process.

Fig 5.6 is from an international recording music company, again examining how its dealers, in this case retailers, evaluate the company's offering. Promotional support, account handling and customer service all come high on the list.

Below in Fig 5.7 we set out a useful format for listing this information in a way that will allow for comparison between the firm that is positioning or repositioning its product and the competitors.

Strength = S or Weakness = W
of the major competitors *(and the relevant products they can bring to bear)*

Key customer choice factors	Your firm	Comp 1	Comp 2	Comp 3	Comp 4
1.					
2.					
3.					
4.					
5.					
6.					
7.					
8.					

FIG 5.7: COMPETITOR REVIEW FORMAT

The data is taken from the product wheel, and set out under the left column. Then, for each of these, an assessment is made of how the service marketer's firm compares with the competition. This is done by indicating, for each of the firms competing, whether the firm is **S**trong or **W**eak, (actual and/or potential)[31].

The service marketer will then build on this using their creative skills, so that the position statement produced follows the following criteria.

It is:

> **WANTED**
> - CREDIBLE
> - UNIQUE
> - COMMUNICABLE
> - DEMONSTRABLE
> - FULFILLABLE
>
> *and is* .... DEVELOPABLE

Coping with emulation

Coping with emulation, i.e. the ease with which a service product can be copied.

The problem

A service may not be patented, nor is it easy to copyright. Any firm is free to copy a good service idea. Indeed, the first indication a service marketer may have that the newly launched idea will be a success is the back handed compliment of the competition launching their own copy.

We see from the late '80s onward how the 'Direct' phenomena has blossomed, from First Direct, through Direct Line and Virgin Direct to Norwich Union Direct etc. etc. Now the rest have to follow or be left far behind. It would be sheer negligence for any service marketer to allow the competition to enjoy a competitive advantage a moment longer than in unavoidable. They must either copy or counter it (as we saw in the example of British Airways' Club Class response to the Virgin limousine).

The only protection is to 'brand' the service product, so that they copyist may not call it by the same name.

Thus in the mid '80s, Barclays Bank launched the first 'Debit Card' branded 'Connect' and within the month it had been copied by Midland with their brand 'Vectra'.

However, branding is an expensive and uncertain strategy as can be seen from the growth of the Directs mentions above.

Some strategies to cope

At first sight the options appear to be fourfold:

1. be first to market consistently, or at least try to be,
2. play 'follow the leader' deliberately,
3. combine the two above as and when circumstances require,

or

4. play 'me too' i.e. move only as a last resort, and then only when forced.

For most marketing people the knee jerk response is to always try to be first in the market. However, unless the firm has the ability (via its technological advantage say) to gain an elongated window of profitability whilst the competition struggles to catch up (as per the Boeing 777 mentioned previously), the balance of risks and penalties do not favor this approach.

The business must generate a considerable number of new product ideas, nurse many of them through the development process, and launch a good proportion of these in order to have one successful new service product (success as assessed by the extent to which its business objectives were attained).

Studies suggest that currently there have to be some 16 service products conceived, to generate one success, i.e. 16:1.

The situation used to be worse, the famous Booze Allen and Hamilton studies of the mid '60s suggested that this ratio was some 58 to one, i.e. 58:1. Marketers are getting better over time but even so the service marketer will still have to throw the dice an average of 16 times before rolling a 'six'.

Thus, any firm opting for a policy of being 'first to market' consistently, must be willing to accept these probabilities for each success and be able to carry the costs of some 15 research and development programs that come to nothing. And all for a very short lead – if the competition are doing their job well.

Over the long run this is a very expensive way to run any business.

Contrary to received wisdom, it is not even certain that in the service sector a 'first to market' policy will generate much kudos for the firm. There is current research[32] that contradicts the strongly held view that such a policy would pay off with market leadership as measured by having the largest market share. The figures now suggest that pioneers (i.e. those firms first to market) often fail in the short-term, whilst those close behind them (early leaders) are more attractive in the long-term.

In the service sector circa 74% of 'first to market' pioneers fail, those that survive only enjoy an average market share of c.10% and they are currently only leaders in some 11% of categories.

The real advantage appears to accrue to those who are early entrants, these firms frequently play the game of 'follow the leader' a skilful halfway house between 'first to market' and 'me too'.

Most current leaders in service markets were not the first in; later entrants often overtake the pioneers (who have been lulled into complacency by being first). Another factor that supports the 'early entrant' is that even where technology provides the lead, barriers to entry are continually falling.

The speed with which competitors can and will copy, especially in global markets, means that there is little time (during which pioneers are uncontested) in which pioneers can build brands, scale-up the service product, climb the learning curve and roll out the service product to mass markets.

It almost goes without saying that for most firms the strategy of 'me too' is unattractive because of the low margins that have to be accepted following in the wake of those who were in the lead. A policy of 'me too' only really works when the firm has the skills of 'value engineering', that is to say they are able to 'reverse engineer' the competitor's service product and develop ways of performing that service at a vastly reduced cost compared to the leaders. Thus providing an enhanced margin, or if cost reductions are passed on to the customers, an unbeatable price advantage.

The most attractive coping strategy

In essence the best way for the service marketer to deal with the inherent freedom for competitors to copy their service product is to play 'follow the leader'.

Simply put this involves:

- A **MANAGEMENT CULTURE** that includes:
  - foresight, and lack of a 'not invented here' syndrome [NIH] i.e. the ability to see the potential in a new idea even though it is launched by the competition,
  - commitment to success, including the willingness to devote the necessary resources to achieve market mastery,
  - persistence, a willingness to keep at it through difficulties,
  - a 'learning environment' that shares knowledge throughout the firm (see opening quote).
- **PREPARATION** consisting of:
  - watching the pioneers like a hawk,
  - knowing the technology of the market better than them,
  - constantly honing the skills of NPD remorselessly and
  - continually squeezing time out of the process,
  - keeping close to customers, husbanding their customer base,
  - close monitoring of the target market's trends.
- **AN ORGANIZATION** that is designed to be flexible, responsive, and able to move rapidly when required.

Then, when the competition launches their new idea, the 'follower' will study everything about the venture, how the service is performed, how customers are responding, how any intermediaries react.

They will consider ways to improve on the new idea, such as reverse engineering to see how it can be done cheaper, faster, distributed more effectively, or for a wider, or for a more specialist audience. The follower will lay contingency plans to strike and then, if the market takes to the pioneer's new idea, they move like greased lightening to get their version to market.

Feedback – taxi exercise

Summary of script employed by Harvey's experience of a private taxi firm in the USA.

Harvey McKay, in his book *How to Swim with Sharks* and *not Lose your Shirt,* tells us of a New York cab firm that in the late 1970's enjoyed some $14,000pa extra tips per driver, (that is over and above what is considered to be the norm by the IRS).

What do they do to warrant this?

The drivers:

- got out of the cab at the start of the journey to let customers in, and at the end of the journey, to let them out;
- gave customers a hand with their luggage, not just loading the cab, but to the front door when unloading;
- were pleasant and courteous throughout the journey.

For the UK this would be the 'expected product', in New York it's revolutionary, but it doesn't end there...

As the customer gets into the cab the driver:

- introduced himself by name, and handed a card to the customer which read:

  "My name is Walter (or whatever) I will take you to your destination in a safe courteous and speedy fashion, please enjoy the journey."

A 'mission statement' from a taxi no less.

As the cab pulled away from the curb, the driver brought the customer's attention to the fact that there was a tray of fruits and snacks in the back for them to enjoy if they wish, compliments of the taxi firm. There was also a rack of that day's papers for them to read should they wish.

Soon after the start of the journey, if the customer was not reading a paper, they are asked if they would like silence or some in-cab entertainment. If entertainment, they were offered the local news channel, local financial channel, or music, they have four kinds, Classic, Rock, Country and Western, and Pop.

As appropriate, the driver would ask whether the customer is new to New York, and if so would they like a commentary on the landmarks they will pass.

To top it all, if the journey originates or concludes at one of the airports, the customer is asked if they would like to arrange to be collected on their return journey, at a special discount fare.

How is that for an 'augmented product'?

References

26 *This is drawn from the paper "The differentiation of almost anything" HBR Oct 1992*

27 *From Hertzberg's theories of motivation. Some call it the so-called "cull test" i.e. the way to reduce a long list of potential suppliers to a short list of suppliers worthy of further consideration.*

28 *For another useful list of sources of inspiration see "Liberation Management" by Tom Peters, section on Market Innovation, "50 Strategies in Pursuit of Luck"*

29 *Times newspapers circa Nov. 1992*

30 *For those interested, the psychologist's name for this is 'Evoked Set', i.e. the set (as in chess set, rather than a set jelly) of data brought to mind by someone making a decision. The advertising industry likes to refer to this, particularly in the area of what alternatives are acceptable, as the customer's 'repertoire').*

31 *Another useful tool of analysis once these eight criteria are identified is the spidergram (See Chapter 4, Part 1, Fig 4.3 of 'Mastering Marketing' by Ian Ruskin-Brown).*

32 *FIRST TO MARKET, FIRST TO FAIL*
Gerard J Tellis et'al, Sloan Management Review, 1996

CONTROL TOMORROW'S COSTS THROUGH TODAY'S DESIGNS
Robin Cooper et'al, Harvard Business Review, Jan-Feb 1996

HOW NEWCOMERS CAN UNDERMINE INCUMBENTS MARKETING STRENGTHS
Clayton G. Smith, Business Horizons, Sept-Oct. 1995

CAN THE BODY SHOP SHAPE UP?
Charles P. Wallace, Fortune 15th April 1996.

SIX

Service is a people business

SIX

Service is a people business

Introduction

"If you are not serving customers your job is to be serving those who are!"

Jan Carlzon – then CEO of Scandinavian Airlines Systems

This chapter examines the essential issues for those who are either in the service sector, or use service as a major way of adding value to their products.

It also addresses how the fact that 'a service business is a people business' has implications on the way the 'process' and customer ownership is managed to the benefit of the organization.

A people based business

As mentioned in Chapter 2, the service industry is a people industry: in a firm where service is all or a predominant part of the product, at least 90% of the employees will meet with customers in the normal course of their work (not counting the 'internal customer' issue).

This is almost the exact opposite of businesses providing just 'goods' alone. Normally in such firms only 10% of the people employed ever meet an external customer, the remainder wouldn't know a customer if they stepped on one and often do not consider that customers are important. (The author has even witnessed a senior designer in a silicon chip manufacturer responding to a complaint that a re-design of a component was taking longer than originally promised, *'not to worry, it's only a customer!'*, he said.)

Service deliverers are 'inseparable' from the service they deliver on the firm's behalf, they are its ambassadors to the marketplace AND because each person is a uniquely different human being, they are 'heterogeneous', and each has the potential to deliver the service in a uniquely individual way.

The service marketer MUST address the two important and inter linked issues of 'Inseperability' and 'Heterogeneity'.

Inseparability

In many cases it matters to the customer which person provides the service. Some times in a general sense, as in the case of a wife of the author's friend who prefers to be treated by a female GP.

And sometimes in a specific sense, in that a given customer may have established a valuable relationship with a particular service deliverer, such as their bank manager, solicitor or accountant.

The issue of which person actually provides a given customer with the required service, gains in importance to customers, the more the product is located toward the intangible end of the service continuum (e.g. care and grooming, through to financial services and professional advice etc.).

Indeed in many situations at this end of the continuum the:

- **service *is* the person, and**
- **the person *is* the service.**

The two are inseparable. This issue can become so important that the customer will feel aggrieved if on occasion they can't be served by whom they wish. The author has a particular hairdresser, a particular chiropodist, he once had a particular solicitor. For him to deal with anyone else in the relevant area is nowhere near as satisfying. To deal with someone unknown means that 'peace of mind' can be sorely damaged.

When in the UK the 'Big Five' banks started to cut back on having a manager in each branch, particularly when they started to 'centralize' those remaining managers into city center locations, the average individual of modest means, and the entrepreneurs of small businesses 'perceived' a severe drop in service quality.

This effect can be so strong that customers will follow their favoured service deliverer when they change employer. Many a firm has lost business by staff taking their customers with them when they leave.

Another facet of this is that many a person has been hired not so much for their abilities in the job, but for the customers they can bring with them when they join.

In some industries like market research, advertising, consultancy etc., this is how: firms set-up from scratch, how firms grow and what often causes them to die.

Many firms have vainly tried to assert their priority of ownership of the customer via terms and conditions of employment, but at the end of the day, the customer will choose. There is only one service sector in the UK where such employment terms are made to stick, where the customer may not choose to follow the service deliverer, at least immediately they change employers. That sector is the legal profession.

The Law Society issues Annual Practicing Certificates, to UK solicitors and UK lawyers which confer on the recipient a right to earn a living practicing law. If a lawyer 'poaches' clients they don't get a practicing certificate for next year.

However, even here it is recognized that if a customer really wants to follow their favorite solicitor to their new practice, and is prepared to wait, there is nothing that the Law Society can or should do to stop it. But, for the solicitor concerned, it had better not be too soon after he/she leaves the former firm, or he/she may be on very 'short commons' for some time to come.

Firms wishing to protect themselves from the undesirable side of inseparability, (the down-side of the customer relationship being stronger with the deliverer than with the firm), have traditionally tried to keep the two from getting too close. In some sectors, market research, advertising, consultancy, junior members of the team are not allowed intimate unsupervised contact with customers, they are cut out of direct contact if possible, or at best only allowed access at junior levels and even then, if possible, only in the company of a 'principal'.

To do this is to stifle initiative, and inhibit the full abilities and talents of the team. And, as in the case with the market research industry, to create the undesirable yet common customer complaint that *"I brief, and get de-briefed by the chief, but it's the indians, who I rarely meet, who do the work,"* which expresses the often felt frustration of not being able to talk to those in the front-line who are closest to the facts.

The above perception also harbors the seeds of doubt that the customer has been charged at the principal's day rate, but the firm has foisted on them someone who is nowhere near as expensive. Not a great way to build trust!!

The ultimate responsibility for building and managing the relationship with the customer is always with the senior people. They do this best by making and maintaining the contacts at the most senior levels themselves. They should make every effort to ensure it is stronger between the firm and the customer than between the service deliverer and the customer.

But even then, the service deliverer who does their job well will be creating contacts that are of value in other contexts. These contacts are portable in the sense that they can be taken with them if, and when they change employers.

So the best strategy to protect the firm's customer base from internal seduction is to make it more attractive for the service deliverer to stay in the firm's employ than to set up in business on their own, or to join a competitor.

However, nothing will stop employees leaving over time, nor customers doing likewise (for this or any other reason).

SO THE ULTIMATE STRATEGY IS CONSTANTLY TO BE GROWING THE CUSTOMER BASE.

Heterogeneity

The issue that the person delivering the service is inseparable from it, is exacerbated via the phenomenon of heterogeneity.

Again, this issue is both a threat, and an opportunity, depending on the service's location on the continuum. The more the service is located toward 'fast food', the more it is a threat, the more toward professional advice, the more it is an opportunity.

At the 'fast food' end of the continuum heterogeneity contains the threat that different people in the team will deliver the service in materially different ways. The firm's 'identity' can eventually suffer if there is little if any commonality across the range of people serving or the service locations, because under these circumstances it will be impossible to build and maintain a homogeneous image for the firm.

At this end of the continuum, businesses are characterized by being in mass markets, i.e. fast moving consumer products where service deliverers are often employed as 'cheap labor'. These employees are most often temporary, part-time, the youngest or oldest in the employed age range, unskilled, less well educated particularly at the 'younger' end and they 'tend' to have a lower commitment than those employees who are in businesses located toward the middle of the professional advice end of the continuum. (The author must stress the **tend to be**. It is not necessarily the case that they are poorer quality even if they do conform to much of the above description. Disney World in the USA gains tremendous employee – cost effective – commitment to the firm and very positive reactions from guests – their word for customers – from the humblest of their 'cast', who are those who clean the park. Tesco's and Sainsbury's, grocery hypermarkets in the UK, obtain superb results via the good work done by their part time checkout, and 'carry-to-the-car' staff). It is all to do with the quality of the managers in charge.

In those circumstances, where the tendency is towards employing 'cheap labour' (in every sense of the word), the management emphasis for these service firms must be on 'regimenting' service delivery[33] especially in the larger, more global firms.

It is important that such a service business should deliver its service in a way that presents a consistent face to its publics. The customer for a burger or whatever should experience an identical service, whether this be delivered in Dubai, in London, in Moscow, or in New York. 'Regimentation' requires a uniform (work wear), a standard operations manual and a high level of supervision, even if only by the commercial equivalent of junior NCOs[34] in the armed forces.

Heterogeneity becomes an opportunity the more the service product is located toward the professional advice end of the service continuum.

These types of services are characterized by the potential for establishing strong relationships between the service deliverer and the customer. Indeed the more to the right (of this continuum) the firm is located, the more success will depend on the existence of a positive relationship between the customer and the service deliverer.

In these circumstances, to build firm positive relationships, it is vital that, between the customer and the service deliverer, there should be little, if any, clash of expectation, personality, culture, lifestyle etc.

The roughest rule of thumb is that people get on best with those whom they consider to be either most like themselves or slightly superior to themselves in whatever way is appropriate, e.g. in intelligence, social position, age or lifestyle etc.

Thus, if a firm's customers are 'pinstripe suited, ex regimental and middle aged' (to cite one stereotype), it is usually a mistake to field a young, casually dressed, trendy person no matter how well qualified they may be. To do so is to invite a clash of cultures or personalities. It will be difficult to do business between the two parties.

If in doubt, the service marketer should suit the horse for the course, send in those who match the customer as closely as is possible.

However, the reverse can also hold true. Firms who supply a service to the 'creative' parts of the advertising industry, or the creative people in software houses have learned that it is generally counter-productive to send in the 'blue suits'. (They don't fit the part.)

But, to come back to expectations, the above is the crudest of paradigms. If the customer is a 'blue suit' and the supplier provides a 'creative' service such as say advertising, graphic design or writing software, there is a strong possibility that the customer will have preconceptions as to the sort of person who can perform these tasks best, i.e. 'expectations'. They know, for example, that *"these designer chappies are a bit like hippies, casual clothes, designer stubble and all that sort of thing"* (to quote another stereotype).

To send in someone wearing a blue suit, no matter how creative his or her talents, is to cause enough dissonance to register on the Richter scale.

Similarly, if say a 'creative hot shop' were looking for accounting services, they would be expecting at least a 'suit', they too have preconceptions.

The ultimate therefore is to know what sort of person the customer expects to deal with, and to match that 'expectation' as closely as possible.

For the large firm, particularly those in business-to-business markets, this is relatively easy; they hire people that will fit with their customer profile, by segment if relevant. That is to say, different segments will each have their own specific teams to deliver the firm's services.

For the smaller firm that would be an extravagance.

In this case the firm will hire people who have either the ability or the aptitude (and then train them) to adapt themselves to the particular culture, lifestyle, expectations et al of the customers to be served.

A head of a major design studio known to the author has a maxim with his team, that the diary, does not just tell you where you are going today, but it should also tell you 'Who' you are GOING TO BE TODAY: On Monday if you are going to supervise the video shoot, you dress accordingly, Gucci shoes, designer jeans, and you drive the company limo. Those prima donnas on location have got to know who's the 'gaffer' (Boss). However on Wednesday, when you go to the firm's bank manager, it's the blue suit, you've got to look dependable.

The service triangle

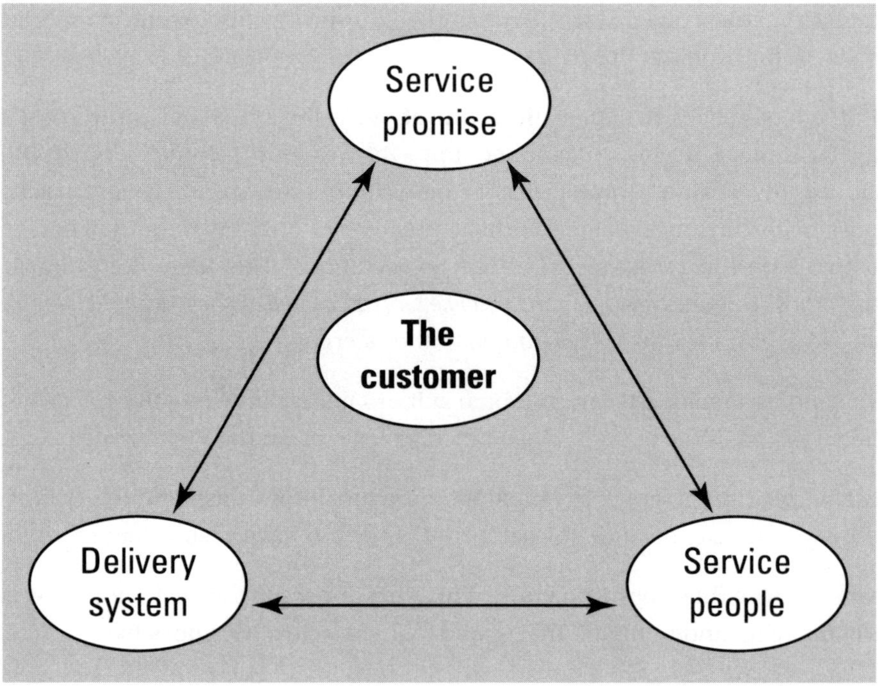

FIG 6.1: THE SERVICE TRIANGLE

Ron Zemke[35], originally suggested the idea of the 'Service Triangle', and we will meet this again in Chapter 8 where the issues of service promise and delivery systems will be discussed in full. For now it is sufficient to say that the 'Service Triangle' is best viewed as a tripod, i.e. something that has three legs which support the customer, remove any one leg and the customer falls off.

Although these 'legs' are seen as being of equal importance they are there to deliver the desired quality service for the customer, and as per the Jan Carlzon quote in the heading to this chapter, there are two types of people, 'those who serve customers, and those who support those who serve customers'.

However, in the main this chapter and this section in particular addresses the third 'leg' of the tripod, 'Service People', i.e. the first category re Carlzon's rubrick those who are in the front-line.

Zemke maintains that those who serve customers should be "recruited for their aptitude as service givers", that is to say they should like looking after the needs of others. Though this is not unimportant at the 'fast food' end of the 'Service Spectrum' – it is critical at the 'intellectual property' end.

Service givers cannot be introverts – nor, in the main, should they be 'show-offs' i.e. those who perpetually desire to be 'center stage'.

The ideal personality type for the person in the front-line of a service business, is one with a strong element of being a 'people person', they must like people, and get personal satisfaction from delighting customers. In other words they should be 'amiables'[36].

Once a member of the team, they should be "encouraged and empowered" to use their initiative where necessary (risky at the fast food end of the spectrum but a critical factor at the intellectual property end). The implication is that one of the criteria for recruitment and when in the job, must be that the ideal service giver should welcome the responsibility, which comes with autonomy.

Service managers should therefore:

- select their teams on this basis, train them to do the job (initial and continuous training) and delegate the necessary authority accordingly;
- generate and live a culture that is tolerant of mistakes. These must be genuine mistakes, in the sense that they were a good try that did

not happen to work[37]. To make a mistake is not a sin, it is a learning opportunity – the sin is not learning from them and making the same mistake time and time again;

- Be trained and well managed – the on-going training support of his or her team should be a major element of the 'front-line managers' job. The dictum is 'Train hard, fight easy'[38]. However, even if the initial training is not necessarily the responsibility of the front-line managers to conduct, it is critical for the manager to ensure that the future team member does get this training, earlier rather than later, and that it is conducted to the highest standards. Through these people, the new team members, and only through them, will the manager be able to attain the targets for which he/she is responsible.
- Be aware and committed to the 'service promise'(i.e. that part of the team mission addressing the customer service of the organization) and its application.

  Again this is the responsibility of the front-line manager to ensure that this happens. It's not a bad thing to remind the team members of their 'mission' at every team meeting – they may get fed-up constantly being reminded, but they will remember.

In addition, front-line people should be:

- set goals and performance standards;
- kept informed of how well (or otherwise) they are performing against them;
- well motivated by suitable rewards.

Those who perform well should enjoy 'recognition'. That is to say they should get a fair level of management attention. (The reverse is often the case where the stronger members of the team are left to fend for themselves whilst the weaker ones enjoy a high level of their manager's time.)

Apropos the above: a common mistake at the fast food' end of the Service Spectrum is to neglect to link cash rewards to high levels of service achievement. It is only in the more up-market restaurants that servers (waiters and the like) get tips from the customers. Even then this activity is becoming constrained in many parts of the world, (about which more in a moment). In fast food outlets and the like, servers get a very low wage, often the minimum and any extra money makes the job a lot more worthwhile for them. The outcome is that the servers are more motivated and committed.

However, there are an increasing number of establishments who are greedy and are adopting one or both of the following systems that work against the server getting a tip.

One tendency in this direction is for the establishment to include a high service charge on the bill – this is supposed to go towards rewarding the staff, so customers ask why should the server get a tip as well? The restaurant practice of regarding this charge as a contribution toward the bottom-line, rather than a reward for the staff – is gaining ground.

The other ploy is for the establishment to insist that all tips are shared, not just amongst the waiters, but also with the 'back room boys', e.g. the kitchen. So why should any one server try harder? Any tip they get will be well diluted, and those waiters who are well below par will get the same money at the end of the evening/week, whatever.

No wonder many firms at this end of the spectrum find suitable well-trained and experienced staff hard to recruit.

Whereas at the intellectual property end of the Service Spectrum it is common for 'partners' to handsomely reward their back room teams who, although they rarely encounter customers face-to-face, will probably have more contact with the customers than the partners, but by way of telephone only.

Finally

- The service teams should be well supported by directors and Managers from the top down. Good management practice can only come from the top of any organization (not just the service sector). This support should be a lot more than platitudes (which breed cynicism), it should be action orientated.

Exercise

As a result of digesting the above, how do you intend to improve:

- your recruitment process for people to join the front-line in your firm?
- your retention policy?
- your policies for rewards and incentives for the best performers in your teams?

  Specifically: what are your intentions regarding cash, recognition and attention?

References

33 *See Script / Blueprinting etc. Chapter 8*

34 *Non commissioned officers, e.g. from Corporal to Sergeant Major*

35 *Ron Zemke is a customer service guru and has authored such books as 'Service America', 'Knock your Socks off Service', and has co-authored 'The Service Advantage' with his colleague, Karl Albrecht.*

36 *From Susan Delenger's 'Geo-Psychometrics' which details five basic behavioural types of person. The 'Amiable' is a 'People Person'. For more information see the excellent video presentation by Susan, produced by CareerTrack International and now marketed by Time Warner.*

37 *These should be genuine try's not 'Brushes with Insanity' as John Cleese has so beautifully put it in his speech 'The Importance of Mistakes' Video Arts publication.*

38 *Marshal Vorishelov, the victor of Kursk, the largest tank battle in the world to date.*

SEVEN

Making the service tangible

SEVEN

Making the service tangible

Introduction

"It is the star to every wandering bark whose worth's unknown, although its height be taken…"

Shakespeare's sonnet 136
'Let me not to the marriage of true minds…'

"You can have good physical evidence, or bad physical evidence, but you can't have no physical evidence!!!"

Anon

It is common knowledge that a service is by its very nature intangible – what is often not realized is that the perception of a service business, at least the first impression a customer gains of it, is strongly influenced by the 'tangibles' associated with the provision of that service, whether these are deliberately chosen by the service provider or not.

This chapter provides the reader with a framework for selecting the means via which the service firm can add a favorable tangible dimension to the business – and – avoid the damage that can accidentally be done to the business by association with an inappropriate type of physical evidence.

Good physical evidence requires that the service provider takes charge of it.

How to 'tangibilise' a service

Many years ago the author had reason to employ the services of a barrister to help evict disruptive tenants from one of the houses he then owned.

Initial contact was by telephone first with the clerk of chambers from which the barrister worked, then with the man himself. First impressions formed by his telephone voice and manners were favorable. When the author visited the chambers the favorable impression was initially re-enforced – the premises were clean, light, airy and traditional quasi gothic. They effectively communicated the majesty of the law to all who entered. BUT when the man himself was first encountered, straight from court and still in his wig and gown, the first thing noticed was that the collar of the shirt he wore under the gown was turned inside out, was frayed, was very grimy from probably being worn in court all that week, it was by now late Friday afternoon.

At that point, any confidence the author may have had in the man evaporated. Was the author's dim view of the man coloured by his background as an ex Royal Marine? Of course it was. Perhaps other clients may not have been quite so sensitive to a frayed inside-out dirty collar. However, one can be sure that the man did not realize the message he was sending, and surely the author could not have been the only one of his potential clients that formed the opinion that this was symptomatic of the level of attention and care that the barrister would pay to the author's case. Another counsel was sought who subsequently won the case with damages – following this the second barrister was recommended to all and sundry who had need of a competent counsel. Even if the author had stayed with the first man, and had won, he would never have recommended the barrister to others lest the author be judged by the barrister's dirty shirt.

Logical? Perhaps not, but that is the nature of how customers react to physical evidence. The assessment of service products is, by its very nature, mainly subjective – very infrequently is it objective. In other words, emotion plays a large part in the perception of the quality of the service provided.

When people are asked what differentiates a service from a 'product' (i.e. a good) the most commonly volunteered answer is that a service is intangible. By which they mean that a person cannot touch, taste, feel or smell it, they can't have a linear measure of a service be that either metric or imperial; a service cannot be weighed, it cannot be either hot or cold. A service can only be measured on one objective dimension (time). All other measures of a service are therefore subjective, i.e. assessment of a service is often a matter of 'taste'. The quality of the physical evidence is like beauty, in the eye of the beholder.

As we can see from the anecdote above, one of the most common indicators people use (often perhaps intuitively) to assess the service on offer is the 'physical evidence' associated with it. This evidence can be deliberately provided by the service business, and/or it occurs accidentally as part of the environment in which the service takes place. The physical evidence must be a deliberate policy of the business, e.g. the tables and chairs, linen, cutlery, crockery and glassware of a restaurant (in addition to, and complementing, the decor of the dinning room and bar).

The service marketer must be sensitive to this issue, and do their utmost to ensure that the message sent is the message they intend to communicate.

Classifying services

In the following figures we see that it is possible to draw up a relationship that exists between the types of service, the typical recipients of these services and the 'natural' tangibility normally associated there with.

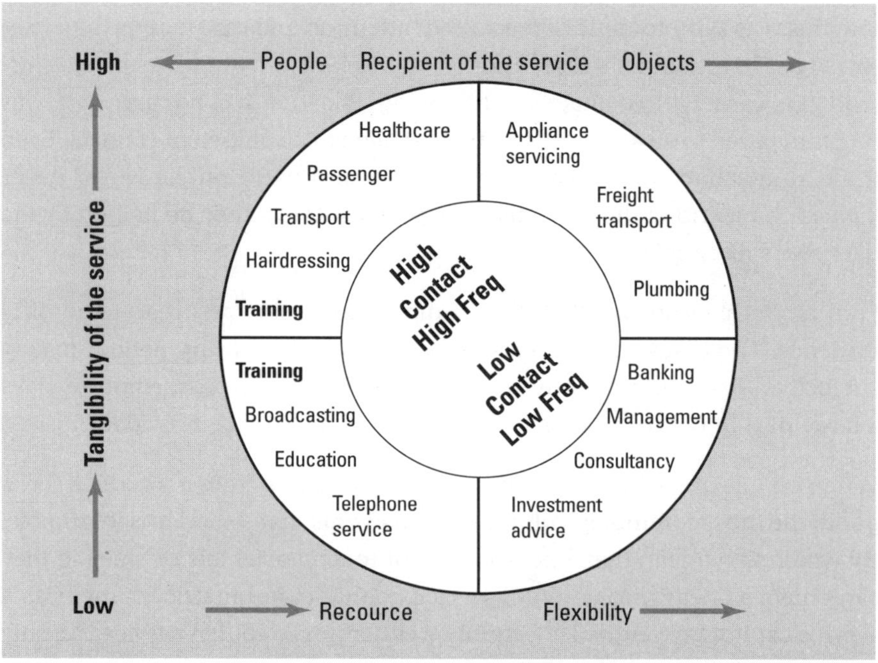

FIG 7.1: A CLASSIFICATION OF SERVICE ENCOUNTER TYPES

In Fig 7.1, we see four main classifications of services.

The vertical axis denotes total intangibility at its base, and at the top, high levels of tangibles naturally associated with the service. Services at the bottom of this dimension are intrinsically intangible by nature and therefore ripe to have some physical evidence associated with them such as books for education, and for telephone services, hand-sets and directories for example.

At the top of this dimension some physical evidence is normally associated with the service such as hospitals, clinics, transport vehicles (logistics and public transport) etc.

Between these two quadrants we see that 'training' falls each side of the dividing line. Business training will normally have a good deal of naturally associated physical evidence, e.g. the training venue, work books, exercise paraphernalia et al.

Below this line the training could well be in the form of a broadcaster leading their unseen audience in keep-fit exercises (as Terry Wogan was once prone to do during his daily music show in the early 1970s – the feature was known as *Fighting-the-Flab*). Nowadays this is done via television, video tape or DVDs of exercise regimes. The physical evidence is the view on the screen, plus the packaging of the physical recorded medium, which can be very creatively customized to add tangibility to the service.

The horizontal axis shows that recipients of the service are to the left of the diagram mainly people, and to the right objects.

Top right, above the horizontal, it is the household appliance, e.g. the central heating boiler that gets the attention, whilst below this line it is the customer's money that is serviced.

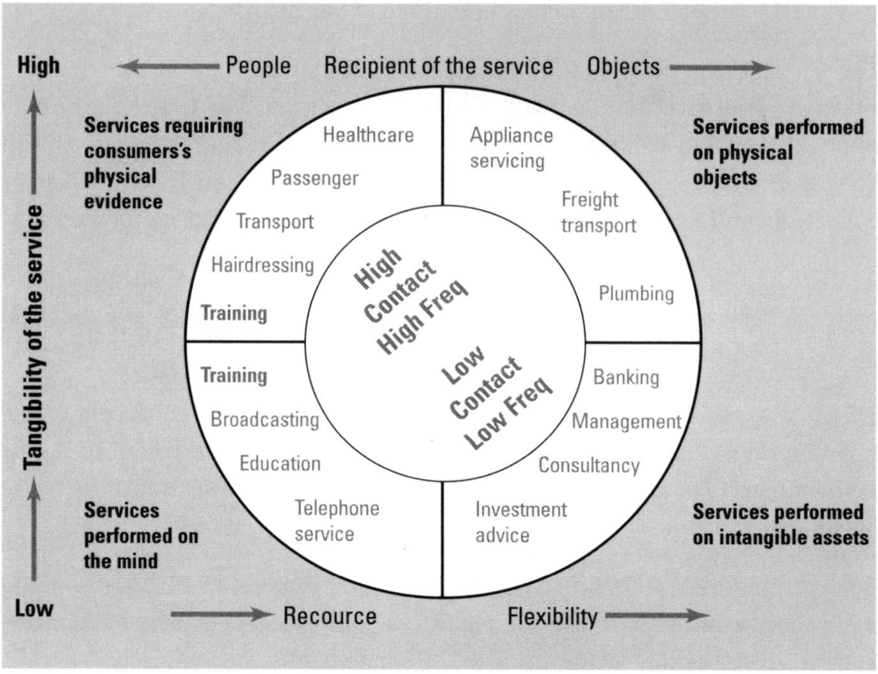

FIG 7.2: A CLASSIFICATION OF SERVICE ENCOUNTER TYPES (ii)

Additionally we can see that the top left quadrant involves services requiring the presence of the consumer during its performance.

Many services fall into this sector. They range from the hospitality industry to transport and education (for the last, at least in body if not in mind). The remaining three of these quadrants identify what the recipient of that service may be.

High customer contact to the top left, low contact to the bottom right.

Finally, we see at the bottom of this figure that the flexibility of resources is indicated. The more to the right, the more flexible the resource management can be, the more to the left, the less this is so. (See Chapter 8 and 9 Process and Managing service resources.)

Tangible / intangible balance

Just as it is not the case that services are totally intangible, neither is it the case that goods are totally tangible – even without the addition of service to provide the competitive differential. A continuum (as per figure 7.3 below) is often used to portray how the ratio of tangibility/intangibility changes as the 'product' moves from raw commodity goods such as crude oil to the esoterics of Professional advice. This changes from almost purely tangible commodity goods such as crude oil, metal feedstock, wheat, cement. at the highly tangible end, through to the almost ephemeral, intellectual property driven businesses, the law, consultancy, tax advice, religion et al, at the other end; as per the following diagram.

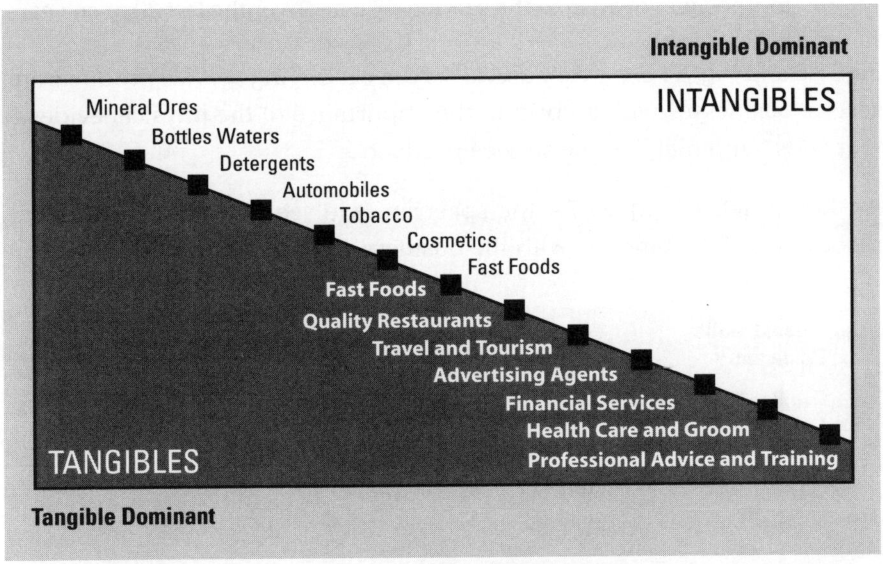

FIG 7.3: THE GOODS AND SERVICES CONTINUUM

In the above figure we see that the conventional divide between what is a 'good' and what is a 'service' is said to be the point where the balance of tangible versus the intangible is approximately 50/50, but how one can measure this, given the subjective nature of the intangibles, has never been satisfactorily explained.

Two things are of note here:

1. The first is that even the most homogeneous commodity good can have associated intangibles which can sometimes be so strong that

they distort the position of that good in its market. Two examples will serve to illustrate:

During the 1939/45 conflict in Europe the British engineering establishment were strongly of the opinion that the ball bearings of the axis forces were superior to their own because their manufacture involved the use of 'special' iron ore from Sweden. The Allies were of the view that to produce the same quality of ball bearings they had to have access to the same Swedish ores. The saga of the extraordinary lengths to which the Allies went in pursuit of this quest makes exciting reading.

2. The second example is the rapid rise in the use of services to add value to otherwise tangible goods. Indeed this can be said to be responsible for the main growth of the service industry over the last 20 or so years.

Figs 7.3 and Fig 7.4 are a very useful way of classifying service products and service businesses with respect to the importance of the physical evidence that adds 'tangibility' to the service product.

At the top left of Figure 7.4 the spectrum, we see that there is a natural association of the tangible with the business.

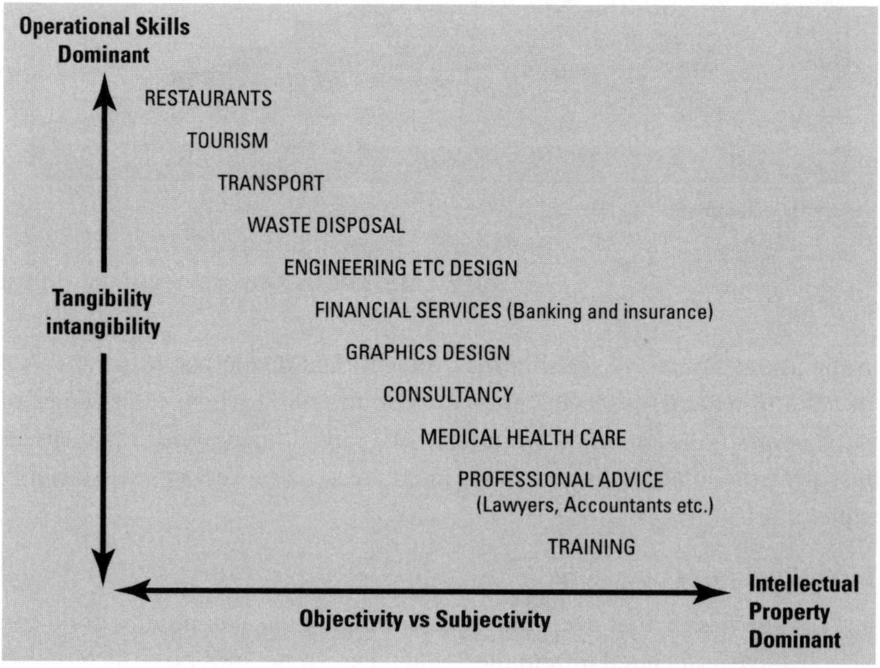

FIG 7.4: THE SERVICES SPECTRUM

For example

1. Restaurants (should) exploit such physical evidence as the décor of the dining room, the quality and style of the table linen, the cutlery/crockery, right down to the layout of the food upon the platter. Other tangibles potentially effecting the customer's perception are, for example, the uniforms of the waiters and other visible staff, the décor and cleanliness of the toilets, the list goes on. And if the chef comes out of the kitchen to greet the diners he or she ought to be in their best whites when they do so.

2. Financial services, banking and insurance businesses etc. often have large and imposing buildings for their head offices. However, with the exception of those banks, which specialize in the needs of the rich, (such as Coutts), the bank's branches, where these still exist, are often 'the poor relation'. Today, and no doubt for some years still to come, these institutions will be cutting costs, closing branches, outsourcing call centers, and doing more and more business via the internet, credit cards, ATMs and direct mail. If they believe to any degree that physical evidence is necessary, it will be provided via the payment cards (be they credit or debit), the documentation associated with the so-called service, or via the increasingly pokey branches that are left after the closure program.

At the extreme lower right of Fig. 7.4 professional advice appears in all its phases, from lawyers through accountancy businesses and business consultants to trainers of all colors and persuasions.

At this end of the spectrum, assessment of the quality of the service provided by these practitioners is almost completely subjective. Additionally many of the service firms at this part of the spectrum are either not allowed to advertise their wares overtly or promotion is severely restricted by their professional bodies. Thus the use of physical evidence becomes disproportionately important to the development of these Practices' business.

So what is the implication of all the above?

This is best expressed in the diagram following:

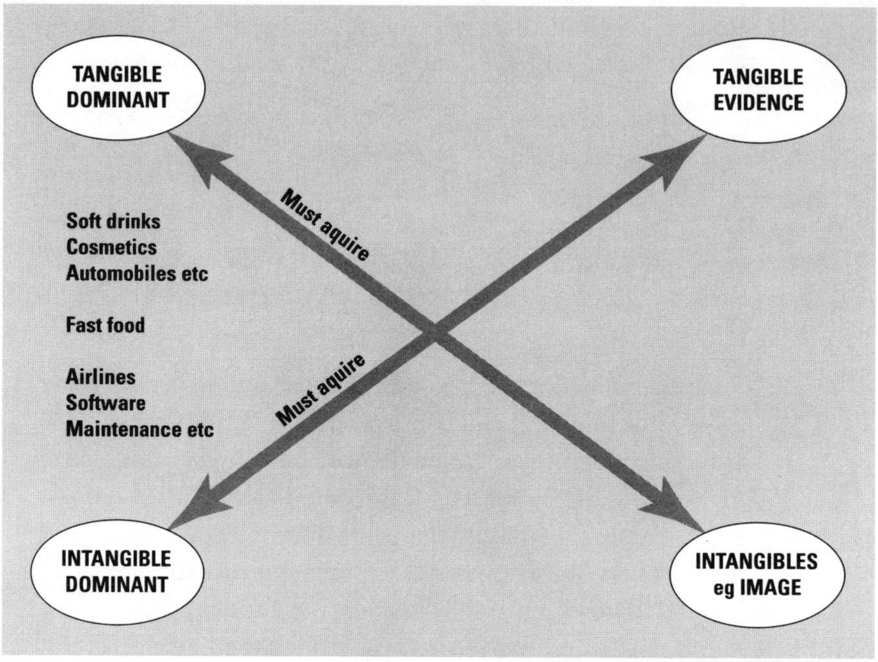

FIG 7.5: MODEL OF TANGIBILITY / INTANGIBILITY DOMINANCE

The message from this figure is that the more the business is tangibles dominant, the more the firm must look to the intangibles to differentiate and progress the business.

Coca Cola is nothing but a cola flavored drink, but the Coca Cola brand is redolent with a plethora of intangible aspects. Not only is it said to be the 'Real Thing' but it is also associated with the younger generation (whatever the year), their mating rituals and fun pursuits, and it wants to be seen as the pinnacle of good taste both in terms of style as well as flavor.

Many people may disagree with this contention, but the purchases of those who do agree make this a very valuable brand. On the other hand, services such as airlines, consultancy and software programs are so intangible that they must be 'tangible-ised' by association with things that the customer can touch, taste feel and smell – in other words physical evidence.

So the savvy airline exploits the modernity and prestige of the aircraft used, the décor of the airplane cabins, and the comfort of the seats especially in Business and First Class.

They also stress the convenience and the prestige of the VIP departure lounges, the limousine service to and from the airports, and all the other little perks such as video on demand, being able to access your emails whilst in flight, make international mobile telephone calls from the comfort of your seat. The list goes on.

Another example is computer software for the home or small office: notice how big the box is in which the necessary media (often a CD) is sold, even though the manual is often on the installation disk. Such small contents surrounded by so much air. But if the box were smaller, the reasoning goes, customers would not feel they were getting anything that warranted the inevitable price charged.

The dimensions of physical evidence

There are three main dimensions of physical evidence:

1. **Function**
2. **History, and**
3. **Aspiration.**

The following illustration puts these dimensions into context:

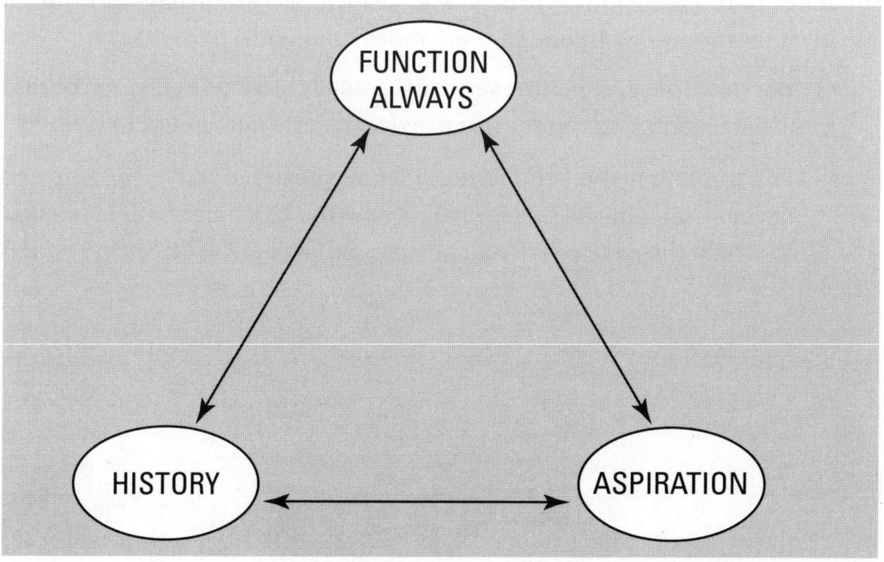

FIG 7.6: THE THREE DIMENSIONS OF PHYSICAL EVIDENCE

The foremost of these dimensions is 'function'. This establishes the legitimacy of the physical evidence. So as to be taken seriously by the intended audience, the tangible items MUST perform some function essential to the provision of the service.

Examples of this have already been given, e.g. the accoutrements of a restaurant.

Further examples are the location size and style of the offices of a professional advisor. Also the car they drive, the clothes they wear, the firm's stationery et al. Additionally we can see the hospitality industry using physical evidence such as the hotel furniture, the bed linen, the printed matter of the hotel services on offer from menus to room guides.

As already mentioned airlines use the actual airplane, the uniforms of the cabin, flight deck and ground crews et al.

Whenever service providers have tried to employ some tangible which has no function in the provision of the service, the customer pays scant regard to them (some years ago there was a trend to give out membership cards which had no 'function' i.e. no practical use related to the service business giving them out. They were not used to gain access anywhere, nor obtain discounts on the service). Experience tends to show that the customer becomes annoyed by these items and they become counter productive to the success of the service business.

The other two dimensions, 'history' and 'aspiration' are usually present in one form or another, with one of them more dominant.

- For the former, either the service is actually steeped in history, or that is the impression the service provider wants customers to have, or
- For the latter, the service provider wishes customers to form the impression that the service will enable the customer to achieve that to which they aspire ("Be all you can be" Army USA).

We show these dimensions beneath the photographs following. In Fig 7.7 below we explain the meaning of the different configurations:

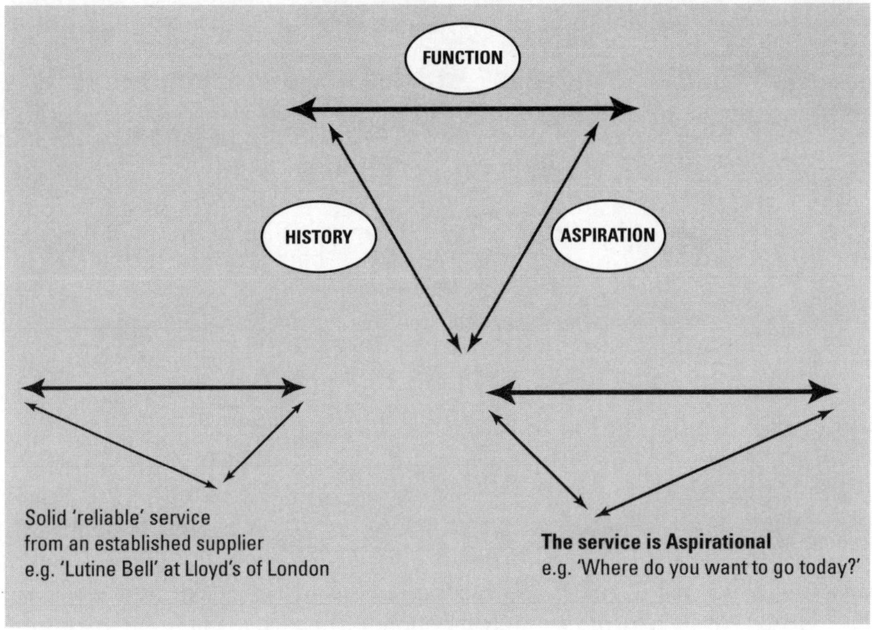

FIG 7.7: THE THREE DIMENSIONS OF PHYSICAL EVIDENCE

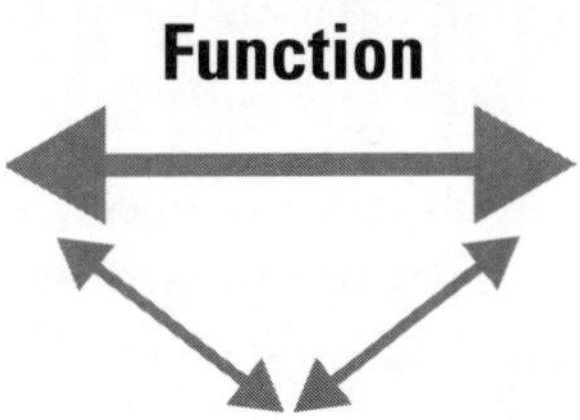

The following pages illustrate this concept with photographs drawn from the every day and occasionally the exotic.

Starting with examples of 'function': the diagram, for the sake of simplicity has the same proportions of history and aspiration, though in all three cases shown this is not the case.

The following examples are of almost pure 'function'. In the last case the items are sending a message, but entirely the wrong one.

FIRST are some examples of paying-in slips from banks and other financial institutions.

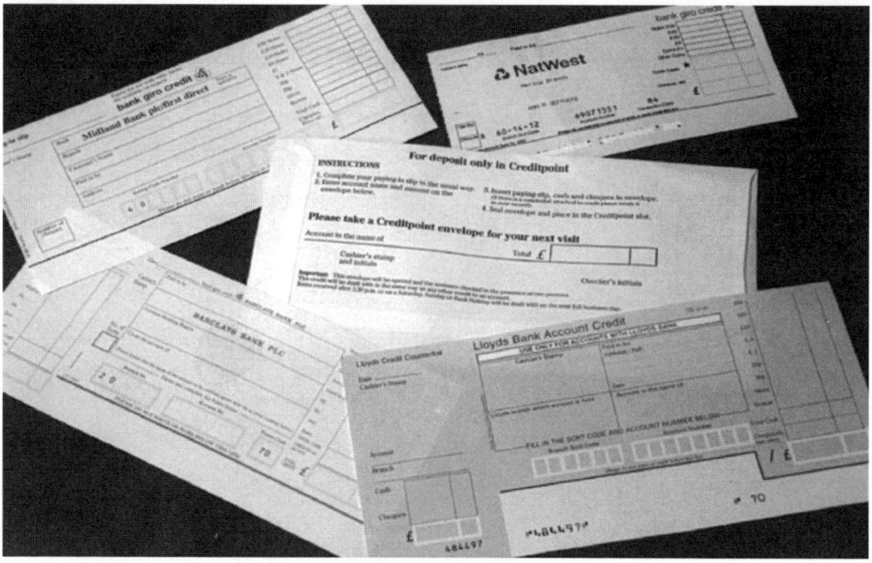

The purpose of such forms is purely functional. There is no intention to impress the customer with the organization's status or modernity.

The forms are there to facilitate the administrative function of recording the amount paid-in, by whom, when, and into what account. And to do this with little fuss, and the minimum chance of error.

The **SECOND** issue opposite is work wear. The illustration shows a collection of 'airside' workers for British Airways. What applies to them, will, to all intents also apply to equivalent personnel for any other airline, and even other jobs where work wear is the norm.

The functions of these clothes are several: from the view of the employer, work wear provides a uniform associating the worker with the firm.

To those customers that see such people from the departure lounge (for example) these uniforms say "you are being cared for by professionals"(a role also encountered in the work wear of health carers).

Another function is to indicate the individual's organizational role both in terms of the job that is done and the authority they may have over others (e.g. foreman, shift manager).

Finally, the obvious, but often least important function is to provide the worker with the means of either protecting them from the work environment and/or not having to use their own clothes

Finally, 'how not to do it!!'

The situation overleaf shown was encountered airside in an airport which, for the purposes of this book, will remain anonymous. The furniture was part of a refreshment facility provided in the luggage hall, so that the weary, newly arrived passengers could have a cup of coffee, or whatever, whilst they awaited the arrival of their baggage. This photo does not tell the entire story. This was not an isolated case for that airport. The whole place was worn out, tatty and dirty. The author took this picture because the first time the situation was encountered it had been drawn to the attention of the café management, and the next time he visited, just over a week later, nothing had been done.

The function was rest and refreshment; the message was that passengers did not count.

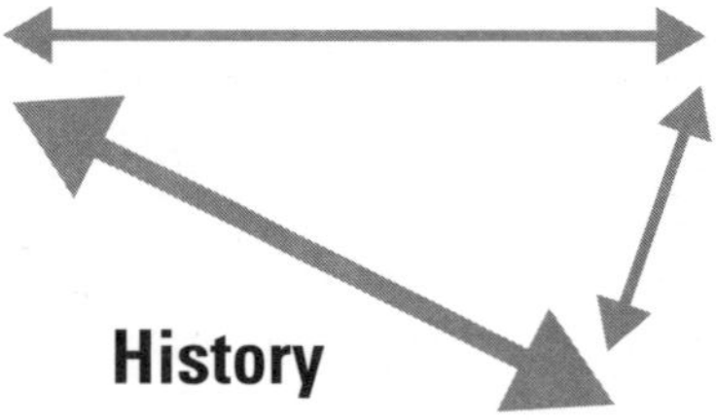

There are several issues addressed via the dimension of 'history'.

One is to create a feeling of dealing with a firm, that is part of the 'Establishment', the creation of 'peace of mind,' and emotional comfort via associating the service with the 'old order', 'Part of one's heritage'. Another is to create confidence in the supplier's ability. A feeling of "They must know what they are doing to have lasted so long".

Still another purpose is to create awe in the beholder – to accept the authority of the Establishment. We see this associated with the 'law' – 'Inns at Court', Law Courts, the Regalia of Judges, the uniforms of the ushers etc. A further manifestation is that of political rulers, monarchies and presidents who often love to surround themselves with historic symbols of power and authority.

Likewise the places of worship for many religions: churches, mosques, Shinto temples, synagogues etc – all wish to be seen as centers of authority. Long has this been the case. The head offices of some modern businesses, such as 'life insurance', are often located in imposing buildings, many of which are hundreds of years old or built to give that impression, they seem to emulate the houses of worship mentioned. Not strange really when you consider the similarities between these two, insurance and religion.

If the reader will permit: Life Insurance asks us to have faith in the company to the extent that as long as we keep up the payments our beneficiaries will be paid in full upon our demise.

Similarly for religion, acolytes and believers are asked to have faith and lead the good life, and in return they will go to heaven when their time comes. What more intangible a service can there be? What greater need is there for tangibility that is imposing to the point of awe?

How else are they to create the emotional trust that they will honor their word. It is very much like the belief in the life hereafter, by the time you know one way or the other it's too late to tell anyone about it. The customer has to take the promises on trust in both cases.

In this photograph we see apparently 'heritage' tourist fodder, but this is not the case. The 'Tudor' style houses featured here are indeed authentic buildings from the Middle Ages, but today they are the offices of insurance agents specializing in the needs of large country estates.

The firms located here must feel that the ambience of these old buildings provides them with a prestige that enhances their standing with clients. That they provide an aura of respectability and reliability for their business. Likewise for firms located elsewhere, if it's not an old Tudor building, it's a Georgian town house in Cheltenham or Bath, or offices in London's Sloane or Berkeley Squares.

Such firms choose 'heritage' buildings for their place of business to provide the benefit of client reassurance.

The ruling establishments of most countries likewise choose grand historic buildings from which to govern. These imply the continuity of the state, the majesty of the role of government etc. Examples are, the Kremlin in Russia and the Palace of Westminster in the UK. Some countries build these monuments to power from scratch, Canberra in Australia, and Washington DC, the Capitol and the White House are well known examples. Indeed Malaysia has built 'Patrajaya' which is a whole new, very beautiful and majestic town outside Kuala Lumpur just to house its government and the service industries, which support it.

However, some rulers today, are more concerned to remind their people of their roots and how far they have come in such a short time. The United Arab Emirates is less than half a century old at the time of writing, the Emirate of Dubai is one of the most modern cities in the world, yet at its heart it features the original Adobe Fort, now a museum, and proudly shows a real Pearl Dhow that was the mainstay of its wealth not so long ago.

Sometimes the previously aspirational can become quickly history in the sense that it has a cachet with which many people will identify.

Take the example of the Concorde (we show it later under aspiration) but at the time of writing it had gone out of service and yet, as can be seen, a model of the historic plane, the first SST (supersonic passenger transport) adorns the main entrance to London Heathrow Airport. History, but very recent history, almost nostalgia. The question is how long will this nostalgic emblem work for British Airways?

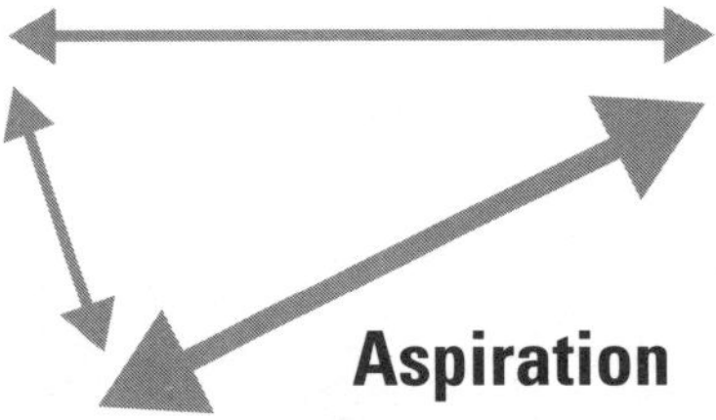

Aspiration

The key here, when marketing a service business, is to have a fair idea what it is that your chosen target market aspires to.

Is it to be modern, upper class, high status, an intellectual, or members of a particular group of people, the list is endless.

The following photographs therefore are nowhere an exhaustive list of the aspirations of target audiences for service businesses. They are just illustrative, using as examples some of the things that some service businesses have used to date.

So we are back to Concorde again.

Note this picture has her in the original British Airways livery.

When she was initially launched, and for some considerable time thereafter, she was the pre-reserve of the really rich and famous.

For almost all of her working life, there was a significant cachet in being able to say that you had flown in Concorde. Such regular flyers would often tell how the main attraction was the ability to get to their destination in a fraction of the time of a normal airplane. However, to them, time was money, and thus how the time saving gained from flying this airplane justified the extra cost. It was not all that comfortable, however, it had a very small passenger cabin.

It was true that the accommodation internally was cramped, but it is still amazing how, during the months leading up to its last flight, people who were not in the 'time-is-money' bracket were so eager to fly on her. So eager that the auction for places on these last flights were fetching more than twice the normal seat price of c.£2,000. Indeed it was rumoured that a few seats on the very last flight fetched £7,000 each.

For someone to be able to say that they have flown Concorde, in the eyes of those who have not, gives that person a real feeling of status and prestige. Will we ever see the like again, perhaps not in this author's lifetime.

Aspiration re prestige does not have to be provided by the most modern (e.g. Concorde), there is also the aspect of luxury. This aspect is found most often in luxury/up market hotels, restaurants and shops etc. such as The Dorchester, Claridges and Harrods.

This aspect of physical evidence, which confers the aspiration of status through luxury, is illustrated well by the resurrection of the luxury train the *Orient Express*. This is not so much a means of transportation, more a means of experiencing the way railway journeys used to be before 1939.

Anyone that wants to get to any of the train's destinations could get there at less cost and greater speed by car, or by airplane. But the Orient Express Company is selling a nostalgic experience of the past.

These photographs illustrate aspects of travel which have long since disappeared from railways.

Consider the physical evidence of the décor inside and outside the train carriage. Boarding the train is an experience in itself.

Afternoon tea is a ritual belonging to the good old days. Regard the accoutrements of the table for afternoon tea, and the level of personal service when tea is taken.

Of course these photographs are from the original promotional material when the *Orient Express* was initially resurrected.

Soon afterwards a film was made of the Agatha Christie novel *Murder on the Orient Express* with a story set in the days leading up to 1939 when the train journey went from Paris all the way to Istanbul.

Other notable aspects of the use of physical evidence for aspiration are the following buildings:

These are the Petronas Towers of Kuala Lumpur, the capital of Malaysia.

They are named after the country's state oil company. It houses some of their most important offices but more importantly it is the site of the Petroleum Club on the floors just above the connecting bridge. Here membership is for the select few, and deals are done over a drink at the bar, or dinner in the superbly panoramic dining room.

Built almost entirely of stainless steel. They were, for some time, a statement of the success, both economic and social, that Malaysia had achieved.

Needless to say that they held the world height record for only a short time. Such towers are a statement to the population and to visitors of the aspiration of the country concerned.

This photograph is of the world's only seven star hotel, the Burj al Arab. At the time of writing this hotel was the pride and joy of Dubai, which is the main city of the Emirate of that name.

The hotel is located some half a mile out to sea, and one either reaches it via a causeway, for which initially there was a fee (refundable on any refreshments taken at the hotel) or by helicopter.

At the time of writing, Dubai had announced that it intended to construct the highest tower in the world. This 'sky-scraper' will be called the Burj al Dubai. Physical evidence for aspiration purposes is another way of considering the cathedrals of the European Middle Ages, as per the example in 'history' above.

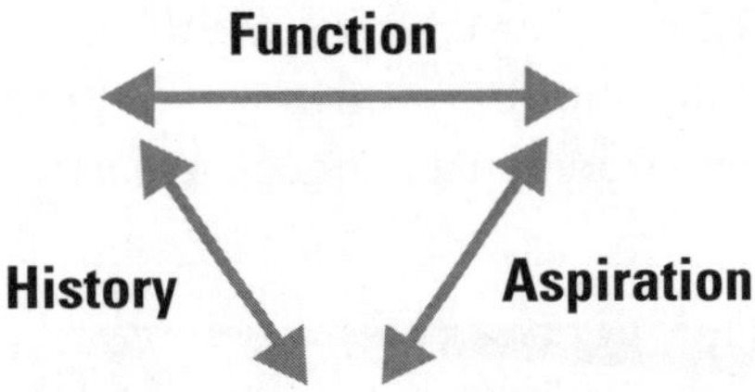

Most if not all of the physical evidence employed in the service industry sector is some combination of all three aspects.

We show examples of this in the newspaper industry. Newspapers, although tangible by virtue of the paper, are not considered to be goods, but service products. People buy them, not for the tangibles, but for the intangibles, the news, the style and quality of the journalism, the point of view of the editorial. All of which is essentially intangible.

In these two photographs of newspapers, taken before many of them went to tabloid format, we see the mastheads (i.e. that part of the front page that carries the paper's title) also we see the typeface the layout and the style and quality of the paper.

The first picture features the *Financial Times, The Daily Telegraph,* and *The Times* (of London). For these three examples, the ambience created is one of 'traditional values' it has been said that "The *Financial Times* is read by those that own the country, *The Times* by those who run the country, and the *Daily Telegraph* by those who think that the country should be run as it used to be run long ago". In short the papers have very traditional baggage to carry.

Compared to the first three, *The Guardian* and *The* (early) *Independent* newspapers above are relatively 'new kids on the block'. Although *The Guardian* originally sprang from the loins of the *Manchester Guardian* it did not become a truly national newspaper until the late 1960s. *The Independent* was launched in the late '70s.

Both take a radical, leftish leaning point of view and their mastheads, typefaces, and layout reflects just this.

Exercise

Here are some final pictures, in each case they are of some aspect of the service sector.

See if you can classify them as to the balance between function, history and aspiration.

When you have done that, consider a short selection of the physical evidence of your own business. What are the main dimensions of each item, is this what was intended, how can these be improved?

Finally, think about all the ways that your business communicates its position on the history vs. aspiration continuum, are you really in control of this, or is it all accidental?

EIGHT

Process (delivering the service)

EIGHT
Process (delivering the service)

Introduction

"It is not what we say, think or believe that matters, the only thing of consequence is what we do"

John Ruskin

This chapter examines the most important difference between services and goods, which is the fact that a service is like beauty, more in the eye of the beholder. It is primarily an experience for the customer and those around them – and this means that it must be seen as a performance by those who are providing the service. As it is performed rather than 'produced', the service marketer must ensure it is well managed. This management is addressed in that element of the service marketing mix referred to as 'PROCESS'. It is said that this aspect of the marketing of any service is a major contributor to building customer loyalty, i.e. turning customers into 'friends and advocates' and as such is so important that it should be allocated a minimum of 50% of the marketer's time effort and budget.

This chapter also includes an examination of how customers and prospects evaluate a service and what actually influences their perceptions of service quality.

Focus on the experience

Marketers of goods (e.g. *motor vehicles*) have very little control over how a customer experiences the use of their product, try as they might to influence this via badging, branding and advertising of the aspirational lifestyle of the stereotypical customer for that model. The marketer's influence is always at several removes from the actuality of the product's use.

The customer of a good is almost invariably out of direct contact with the firm producing and/or supplying that good when it is used. Whereas:

- A service product IS the experience that a customer has when the service is being delivered either to them, or in their presence, to their neighbour.
- A service is no more, and no less than this experience.
- A customer's perception of this experience is THE MOST CRITICAL aspect of its marketing.

The customer's favorable experience of the delivery of that service, confirms that they made the right choice of supplier, and promotes the possibility that they will return to this supplier when next they are in the market.

Favorable perceptions will create and build relationships, unfavourable ones will destroy them. So important is this 'experiential' aspect of a service that it has been rightly named 'The Moment of Truth' (Jan Carlzone, Scandinavian Airlines System [SAS]). During this 'Moment of Truth' all the effort taken to deliver the service either comes to fruition, or is wasted.

Whether it does bear fruit or not of course depends on the customer's perception.

The importance of perception

Whatever we do as business people, the customer or prospect will view our service in their own:

"…unique, idiosyncratic, emotional, erratic, irrational – and – at the end of the day, totally human terms. Perception is all there is."

Tom Peters

The customer's perception will be formed from their perspective, not ours.

All marketers must strive to manage the perceptions of their customers and prospects. However, for the service marketer this issue is vital to the extent that a major part of the service marketer's job has been described (by Tom Peters again) as 'the strategic management of perception'.

BECAUSE: it is the perceptions of the 'prospects' and 'customers', not our perception, that will drive their behaviour.

The wise service marketers will therefore devote at least half of their energy, attention and budget to ensuring that the performance of their service delivers the optimum experience to the customer and turn as many of them as possible into 'friends' and 'advocates' and thus grow their business.

The element of the services marketing mix that covers this aspect, the performance, is process.

SERVICE QUALITY – PROCESS and its MANAGEMENT

THE HURDLES

As mentioned in Chapter 1, the value equation can be expressed as:

QUALITY = PERCEPTION *minus* EXPECTATIONS

Such that where perception is the greater, the customer is delighted, and where expectations are not met, the customer is disappointed, and cannot be expected to buy again.

It is vital for the service marketer to manage this equation. Therefore, in order to manage the equation competently the reasons for possible mismatch between expectations and perceptions must be identified, and understood.

These mismatches commonly arise because of one or a combination of the following causes:

- Expectation misconceptions, i.e. the service marketer imperfectly understands what the customer expects, in that what is salient to the customer has not been identified, (see Chapter 13).
- Resource inadequacy, i.e. there is either an unwillingness to provide the necessary capacity/quantity of resource, or an insufficiency of planning both in terms of the capacity of resource required, and/or how this is to be managed throughout the swings of the business cycle.

- Poor delivery skills, i.e. there are not sufficient of the required skills amongst the workforce, in particular those who are service deliverers. Poor recruitment, training, motivation and management in the front-line being the most common causes.
- Marketing promotion has over promised, i.e. too much hype, and too little ability to fulfill.

A main role for the promotional activities of a service business must be to manage expectations, so that these shortfalls do not occur.

However, there is no point in offering a level of service below that which the customers considers to be the 'norm', and these expectations are always growing. The trap is that every time a customer's expectations are exceeded, this new level becomes the norm, the 'expected' for next time. Thus the expectation hurdle is always ratcheting upward.

Additionally, customer expectations are constantly being affected by the competition, and, (unfairly, or so it seems) by their experiences of being served outside the industry sector concerned. The customer's experiences whilst traveling, say, in the USA, or to Disney, or via a particularly good airline, are often used by them as a yardstick against which totally unrelated services are compared. Therefore, it is vital for the service marketer never to forget that 'yesterday's luxury, rapidly becomes tomorrow's necessity'.

What a customer may want from a service

The general categories of criteria via which a customer may evaluate a service are as follows, the customer could employ any one or a combination of the following 'wants':

- **Reliability,** the service is consistent, dependable and perhaps backed by guarantees.
- **Accessibility,** provided at convenient times and locations with little waiting.
- **Credibility,** the firm and its staff are seen to be trustworthy in terms of delivering what they promise, and with a respectable track-record in their business.
- **Prestige,** the source/supplier is well respected by the customer's peers, and at least there will be no disrepute to the customer's image, at best this will confer status by association.

- **Security,** there will be no financial or other risk to the customer.
- **Privacy,** the customer's confidentiality, and/or person will be respected.
- **Responsiveness,** the speed and attention given to the customer's needs, requests, questions and/or problems.
- **Competence,** the service deliverers' level of relevant skills, know-how, expertise.
- **Communication,** how well do the service deliverers interface with the customer, how accurately and clearly is the service described? How well do they feel that the service deliverer(s) listened to them?
- **Courtesy,** the pleasantness/friendliness of the service deliverers toward the customer.
- **Stress free,** i.e. freedom from physical and/or mental stress, the customer feels welcome, feels 'at home' when dealing with the service provider.

Focus on the performance

The 'blueprint'

To ensure that the performance of the service is optimal, the service marketer starts by designing the experience they wish the customer to have whilst consuming that service.

However, this does not mean just 'Customer Service' (alias customer care et al). Service 'process' is much more than this.

An analogy is the way that promotion on its own (advertising, public relations, sponsorship etc.) is not marketing, yet is a vital part of it. Similarly customer service, is by no means all that there is to the service sector, but it is a vital and indispensable part of it[39].

The proficient service marketer will produce a description of what is required to happen, a 'scenario', a 'blueprint'. This will be based on:

- what is known to be important to the customer (we list some of these things at the end of this chapter, but also see 'saliency, in the context of qualitative research Chapter 12),
- the required 'strategic emphasis' for the customer experience, i.e. Should it be primarily experienced as:

  'Smooth efficiency',
  'Interpersonal warmth',
  Conferring status/prestige on the customer,
  or
  'Nothing is too much trouble'

This emphasis will set out what the customer should experience during service delivery.

The design of the MoT Blueprint[40] will be constrained by the nature of the service being provided along the lines suggested by Lovelock, following:

The Lovelock Matrices

Useful insights into the classification of service products is provided by Lovelock in the *Journal of Marketing*[41]. He expresses these insights via four types of matrix – we show each of these in turn, with examples in each cell to illustrate.

How service is delivered

Types of interaction	Service outlets: Solus	Service outlets: Multiple
Customer visits service outlet	Leisure centre Hospital GP's practice Hairdresser	Passenger transport Print shop Estate agents
Service provider visits customer	Landscape gardener Plumber	AA/AAA/RAC Postal deliveries
Neither directly meet	Credit card Tele-banking etc	Telecoms provider Mail order

After Lovelock ***Journal of Marketing****, Summer 1983*

FIG 8.1: HOW SERVICE IS DELIVERED

The way a service is 'delivered' can yield advantageous insights:

- Is it better to deliver the service via a single (solus) outlet, or via many?
- What is the most convenient form of 'interaction/transaction' for the customer? Is it face to face, or remote such as via mail, telephone or internet?
- How would a change in this type of interaction affect customer perception of quality? (e.g. where can the association of some 'tangibility' be used to best advantage – your site or theirs?).
- If the service must be taken to the customer are there suitable strategies and intermediaries available (e.g. franchise)?

The style of the relationship

Nature of service delivery	Relationship type: Member	Relationship type: Informal
Continuous	Credit card Insurance Public utility	Health service Police
Discrete transaction	Book club Record club Season ticket	Tool hire Baby sitting

After Lovelock ***Journal of Marketing****, Summer 1983*

FIG 8.2: THE 'STYLE' OF THE RELATIONSHIP

It is useful to understand the 'style' of the relationship that exists (or is intended to exist) between the firm and its customers. By 'style' we mean whether the customer's relationship with us is formal and whether provision of the service is in terms of either discrete transactions or is it a continuous process, extreme examples of which would be a health care service (continuous) versus tool hire (discrete).

A continuous relationship where customers can be treated as 'members' (either by mutual agreement or formal contract) is advantageous to the service provider. This provides the opportunity to build a dossier on the customer, and by using this information, strengthen the relationship (via improved service, better segmentation etc.), this raise barriers against competitive entry.

The key issues to be addressed by the service marketer are:

- How best can the firm take the relationship from informal to formal. It can for example, persuade:
  - casual users of a restaurant to dine at this restaurant regularly,
  - firms that use a photocopying/printing services to give the provider all their business.
- What trade-off can exist between pricing and usage rates, e.g. season tickets, money off repeat holidays with the same travel agent?

How much can the service be customized?

Frequency of demand fluctuations

Peak demand	Low	High
Delay often encountered	Computer help Internet bureau	Theatres Hotels Passenger transport
Delay in meeting is rare	Tele-banking Tele-insurance	Public utilities Ambulance service Fire service

After Lovelock ***Journal of Marketing****, Summer 1983*

FIG 8.3: HOW MUCH CAN IT BE CUSTOMIZED?

A key issue facing those who design the process element of the service is the extent to which there is room to allow service front-line staff to exercise their discretion (judgment) in how, and to what extent the service can be tailored to better meet the customer's needs (i.e. customized).

This will impact on the specification used when selecting service-providing staff and how they are to be trained, empowered and managed.

Issues to be addressed in this context are:

- How useful would it be to 'regiment' and via standardization and down-skilling, benefit from economies of scale?
- Will flexibility in customization help us reach more and different types of customers?
- Can we better exploit our staff skills by updating the current service?

In response to these questions, a jobbing builder may specialize in conservatories and patios; a marketing consultancy may specialize in (say) the financial services arena etc., whereas a travel agency could expand their range away from package tours to include tailored adventure holidays for small parties.

The move toward customization can cause friction between operations and marketing. The first wishes to reduce complexity and thus costs via standardization, the second wishes to improve revenue and market share via providing additional value for the customer, and attracting more of them. In addition, higher levels of service will require more empowerment, skills and thus training for those who deliver the service (e.g. a bespoke tailor requires more skill in measuring and fitting than does a shop assistant tending ready made clothing 'off-the-peg').

Also the level of customization will tend to create friction between the marketing and operations function. Service market managers will often see the need for a high level of customization, which poses greater demand on operational staff. Higher levels of service customization often requires employees at the point of service delivery to make decisions based on their own judgment. This means that some employees will require greater levels of training and a wider skill base. For example, a waiter who prepares at the customer's table requires a higher level of training than one who just delivers food from the kitchen to the table.

What is the nature of supply and demand for the service?

Peak demand	Frequency of demand fluctuations: Low	Frequency of demand fluctuations: High
Delay often encountered	Computer help Internet bureau	Theatres Hotels Passenger transport
Delay in meeting is rare	Tele-banking Tele-insurance	Public utilities Ambulance service Fire service

After Lovelock ***Journal of Marketing****, Summer 1983*

FIG 8.4: THE NATURE OF DEMAND FOR THE SERVICE

Are demand fluctuations frequent or infrequent and when they occur are they large or small, and can peak demands be met relatively easily? (See fig. 8.4 above).

As was stated earlier, a service cannot be stored, so if demand exceeds supply this increases the risk of disappointing customers, and this is as good as extending an invitation for another supplier to step in. This makes it important for service managers to understand demand patterns over time. They must know why and when peaks occur, and take steps to work out what alternative strategies might be used for 'smoothing' them. Some examples of how this works in practice would be:

- a DIY store increases capacity via 'weekend staff'
- a transport operation uses price to move demand off peak
- restaurants provide a reduction for early evening diners during the week, but restores normal pricing at weekends.

Typical of the questions that supply and demand fluctuations will prompt in the minds of service managers are:

- How susceptible to peaks and troughs is the business?
- To what extent can peaks be coped with?
- Should alternative strategies be adopted for creating capacity?
- Should alternative strategies be adopted for introducing differential pricing?
- Should a new mix of strategies be experimented with, involving both capacity and pricing?

Coping with demand fluctuation can cause serious problems for service managers and operations managers. Computer technology helps delivery scheduling for services. For example, on the underground train network in Singapore, the passenger flow is constantly monitored via a computer-linked ticketing system. If passenger flow suggests additional trains are required, the system will immediately trigger action to correct the situation.

A classification of service encounter types

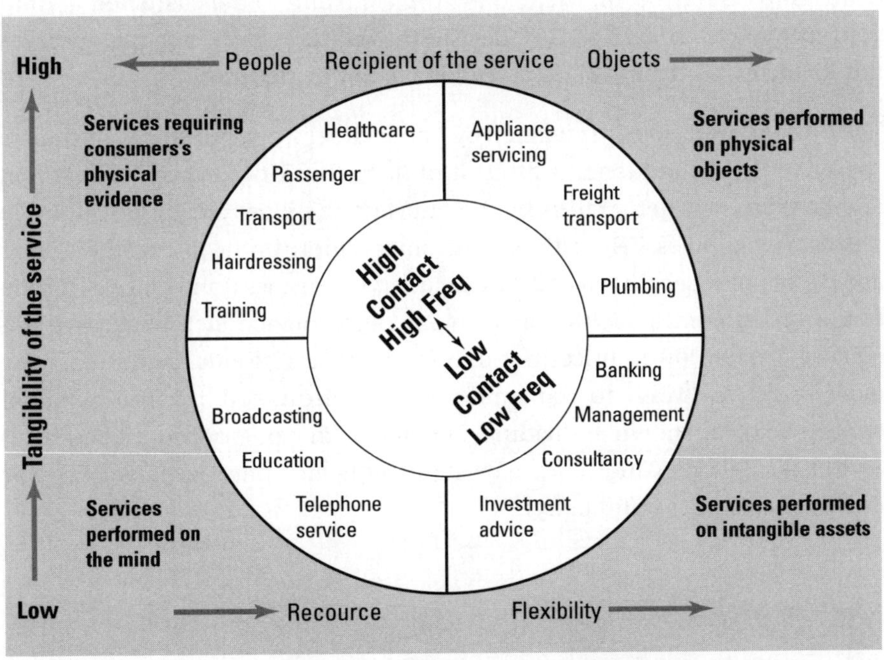

rom: Adrian
almer 1994,
*rinciples of
ervice Marketing*
ve also saw this
Chapter 7,
aking the
ervice Tangible)

FIG 8.5: A CLASSIFICATION OF SERVICE ENCOUNTER TYPES

In this classification system Adrian Palmer contrasts the extent to which a service is tangible (vertical axis) with whether the service is performed on the customer's person, or the customer's property.

For services to the right side, the customer does not have to be present at the same time as it is delivered, to the left s/he does.

The bottom left quadrant is interesting in that customer and provider can be remote one from the other, and there is a trend to move some services from the top left to the bottom left, frequently via employing information technology. So training (as opposed to education)[42] is said to be moving more and more toward 'distance learning' via interactive CD-ROM based technologies.

For services located in the top right quadrant, the provision of the transport, plumbing, vehicle repair etc. is, as seen in Chapter 5, the 'generic' product, and unless it goes wrong, is taken for granted. The really important aspect of these types of services is the manner in which the firm handles the customer contact at the 'before' and 'after' service encounters. On the one hand, this emphasis is needed for those requiring high levels of interpersonal skills when dealing with customers. On the other hand, the spatial and temporal divisions allow a larger than average level of flexibility. For example, the car dealership can collect and return the car from and to the customer, adding customer convenience. It can also service the vehicle at its workshops wherever it is located which maximizes convenience to the provider.

The bottom right corner is typified by financial services: little if any customer presence is required (and as a result of home banking on the internet and tele-banking, it is getting less by the day) and there are almost no naturally associated tangibles. Left as it is the customer is more prone to treat the service as a commodity (see Chapter 12, Pricing a service business) and make decisions based on outcomes such as investment performance etc., which are the equivalent of the lowest price. In this sector of the service industry the marketer must search for ways to economically maximize tangibility and personal contact, e.g. a known individual familiar with your account (personal) and/or a smart banking binder for statements etc., plus perhaps a regular lifestyle newsletter (tangibility).

Variability/flexibility

As the customer performs a service in real time, simultaneous to its consumption, it is flexible and has the potential for a great deal of variability. This is both a strength and a potential weakness.

In some sectors, particularly mass consumer markets, the service marketer may require to deliver a uniform service across the business outlets, maybe even across countries. This will particularly be the case where customers will frequently encounter the service in different parts of the world. Examples to illustrate are say: express couriers, hotel chains, fast food outlets (yes they are a service rather than a good, though they are at the cusp between the two, who would ever visit one for a balanced diet?). In these cases the service marketer will want to present a consistent image wherever they may be encountered.

Notwithstanding the need to empower the service deliverer to solve customer problems and react to the different customer personalities and situations (within defined limits), the emphasis must be on uniformity. This is because the image of service businesses must be consistent across outlets, and this is not served if the various outlets all provide the service idiosyncratically, perhaps even varying its delivery on a whim, or on a day to day basis.

However, in some markets, such as hairdressing, the law, management training, and consultancy, the ability to vary the script according to the needs of the particular customer is a great asset. For these categories of service business it will also prove beneficial to hire people specifically for their ability to 'fit-in with' specific target groups of customers, a sort of 'type casting', sometimes referred to as horses for courses ' (see Chapter 6).

Script detail

Thus, following on from the above, the detail into which this script should go will depend on the amount of discretion and empowerment the service marketer feels able to give the front-line people in their team. The amount of discretion (etc) will, to a large part, depend on whereabouts that service is on the 'Services Spectrum' (see Fig 2.2, Chapter 2).

The more a particular service is located towards the 'intellectual property' end of the spectrum, the more discretion and empowerment it is natural for the service deliverer to have (even need) and therefore the less detailed the script. (The service deliverer being that front-line person who is in direct contact with the customer, even if only by telephone, mail or e-mail.)

The more the service is located toward the operational skills end of the spectrum, the more the detail should be specified. However, this requires skilful management, the art is to get the service deliverer to buy-into the performance criteria whilst at the same time being willing, empowered, able and motivated to use their initiative. This is not done via persuasion alone, the service deliverer has to perceive real support in the form of adequate systems, and the absence of a blame culture if they get it wrong.

The service blueprint

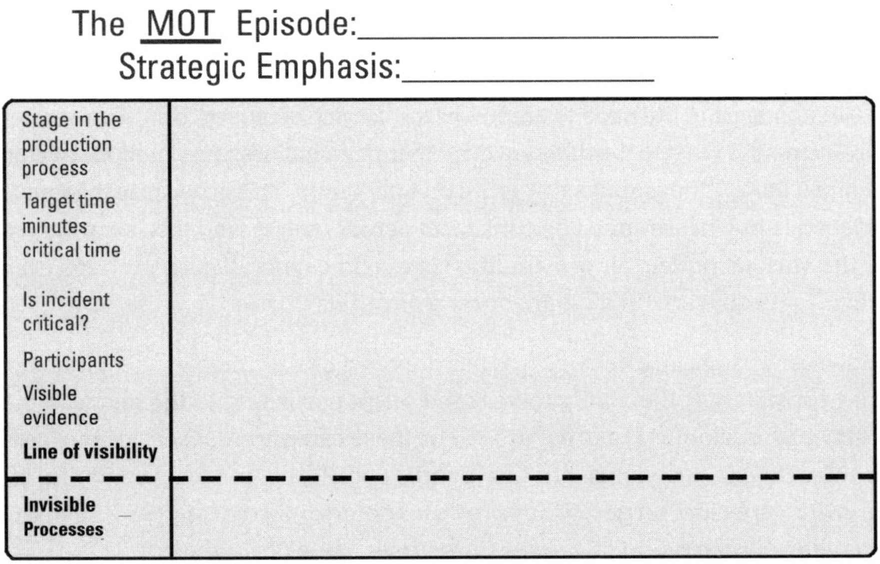

FIG 8.6: THE SERVICE BLUEPRINT

There are critical 'moments of truth' in any service encounter, and it behoves the service manager/marketer to ensure that these are choreographed and scripted so that everything for these MoTs is worked out in advance and nothing gets in the way of a successful service episode. Fig 8.7 is suggested as a useful tool to that end. The horizontal axis is a time line, and the vertical axis indicates the various issues to be addressed.

- Top of the list is an enumeration of the stages within the MoT which have been identified as critical to its success.
- Next is 'time'. This aspect is usually a critical dimension of service (and the only one that can be measured objectively). The metric here

is duration of that part of the MoT episode stating the best time it should take, and the maximum time it can take.

- For each element of the MoT, the degree of criticality is indicated here. The issue is that if this is wrong, then the whole or a major part of the customer's experience of that MoT will be damaged.
- The last two rows are to indicate the major players and what physical evidence is associated with that MoT.
- Beneath the line of visibility are all the backroom activities that are indispensable in supporting the episode, stage by stage.

By way of illustration we show below a fairly simplistic 'blueprint' of an MoT episode of what should happen from the moment a customer arrives at a 'tea shop' to them getting their cup of tea.

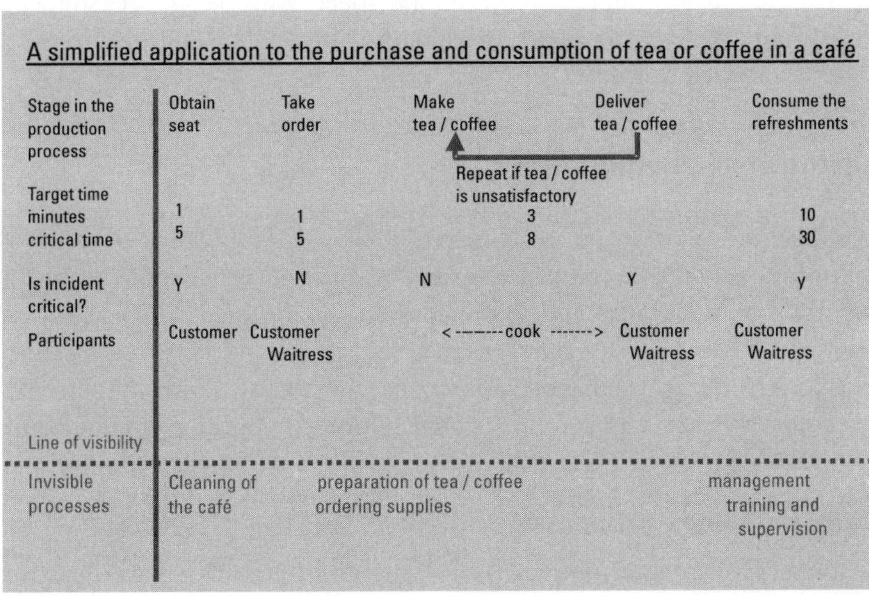

FIG 8.7: CUSTOMER SERVICE BLUEPRINT

Action standards

An important ingredient of the script is a set of action standards that will act as the core behaviors necessary to deliver the desired experience to the customer.

These will consist of actions that can be measured and/or monitored, ranging from:

- the apparently trivial. Such as the frequency with which a customer's name is used. How appropriately was it used, how speedily was the telephone answered, how long is the telephone queue at any one moment, was the agreed (proper) form of words used when answering this telephone; when in a face to face encounter, was eye contact appropriately made etc.

  to:

- the more significant, such as the speed with which a customer's inquiry was answered, the length of time it takes to complete a standard task etc.

Customer participation

It is important that the script involves the customer.

Services should not be considered as being 'done' to a customer, but 'in co-operation with' a customer. Customers should be considered as active participants in the service, the more they participate, the more they feel they have control over what is happening, and the more they will 'own' the outcome. The script therefore should promote maximum positive customer interaction.

Inter-customer influence

Customers will interact with each other whatever the service marketer does. The service marketer should aim to exert influence, if not actually control on this interaction because it is a main source of information to the prospect and customer whereby they form perceptions of the quality of the service provided.

Where the service is 'consumed' in a social context, i.e. customers and/or prospects are physically present with other customers at the same time, this interaction will be continuous even if only passive. Customers will inadvertently and much of the time subconsciously pick up cues from those others present, and from this form a perception of the social acceptability of the gathering which, in turn, will effect their view as to the quality of the service ("Is this for people like me, am I with my peers, or out of place?" or "Is that other customer one of us, what are they doing here?").

This phenomena is well known in the airline industry where, as a consequence, great care is taken when they are required to upgrade people from the back of the plane to Business Class. The check-in staff will be at pains to select those people who will not appear out of place in Business Class, and thus will not cause the person they will sit next to, to resent their presence (they will probably not even know, unless the 'upgrade' spills the beans), because the upgraded person only paid a fraction of the Business Class fare, and yet gets all the perks.

A final example of good marketing management of this phenomenon of 'inter customer influence', is how the good restaurants will be careful to ensure that:

- They 'dress' their window (if and as appropriate) so that the restaurant never appears empty.
- People providing the service are dressed appropriately to the time of day.
- Customers will be segregated into smoking and non-smoking areas as per their preference.

Support systems

The quality and consistency of any actions to deliver the desired experience will critically depend on the internal support that is provided to the service deliverer.

It is necessary to design these support systems in the light of the script, and to ensure they are adequately resourced, with a workable resource/capacity management strategy.

The worst situation is to have a great script, a well motivated and trained service team of deliverers, and (at least initially) eager customers, only to be let down by the capacity of the support system.

For example, this is frequently the case with the 'hotline' of a major 'direct supplier' of PCs that the author knows personally. Here the support systems are so under resourced that customers frequently find themselves having to wait upwards of one hour in telephone queues before they can talk to those from whom they require help. Imagine the frustration experienced by the customer, as frequently is the case, when this is compounded by the customer eventually discovering that they had been allocated to the wrong queue, and that now they have to go to the back of another queue to talk to the right person. This, because of a mistake that was made by the original telephone receptionist due to the pressure of heated customers' complaints.

Is it any wonder that this supplier's once pre-eminent position in direct supply of PCs now needs to be propped-up by ridiculously low prices.

Training

As in any other field of human endeavor, it is irresponsible to empower people to make critical and perhaps expensive decisions, without providing them with the necessary skills. These skills will fall into two categories:

- those interpersonal skills, in addition to the specified action standards, that are generally good practice and applicable throughout the service sector, such as how to handle an irate customer and how to discover the real reason behind a complaint, and
- those that are industry, service situation and/or script specific, such as how to design a mortgage to best suit a customer's particular circumstances etc.

Both sorts of skill require initial training; no one is born with them.

They will also need constant re-enforcement by the service equivalent of the pilot's 'check flight' and follow-up.

Once the script is constructed, the second category of skill can be defined, standards specified, and training programs to impart and to maintain can be designed AND implemented.

Motivation

The 'engine' that makes the script work is the motivation of those who are delivering the service be they dealing with internal or external customers.

This motivation can be either extrinsic, or intrinsic.

The former, consisting of things like 'employee of the month', 'bonuses', 'pay for results' et al (usually based on some measure of customer satisfaction) is easy to implement and measure, but expensive and short-term.

The latter is difficult to implement and measure, but is very low cost, promotes employee loyalty and is long-term.

Control

As in all other fields of management, control requires the input of the right information, and the access to effective channels, whereby the marketer can influence and correct behavior as required.

The information required by the service marketer, consists of feedback on:

- How well the specified action standards are being performed in terms of skill and consistency of application, and
- What is the effect this is having firstly on customer satisfaction levels, and secondly on customer retention and advocacy.

The former is obtained via such tools as internal audit, and mystery shopping; the latter via the Marketing (or Customer) Information Systems [MIS or CIS, these being discussed in Chapter 13].

Channels of influence are not obtained by Fiat. No commercial organization in the service industry can be successful if run as a dictatorship. The service marketer must therefore constantly conduct a program of 'internal marketing'. This is because the service marketer's most valuable asset is the internal political support of those on whom he/she relies to deliver his/her script. Without that support, all the brightest ideas in the world will come to naught.

A major skill in this pursuit must be the ability to sell the script upward and downward in the organization. In both directions the process is mainly informal, and is greatly assisted by the practice of 'Management by Walking About' [MBWA].

The service marketer must consider it imperative to make the maximum number of connections internally as is possible, never forget the axiom that "He who has the largest rolodex wins" (this is not gender specific, it applies to women as well).

Promise and delivery: Checklists

This is all summed-up in the Service Triangle suggested by Ron Zemke, which we saw earlier in Chapter 6.

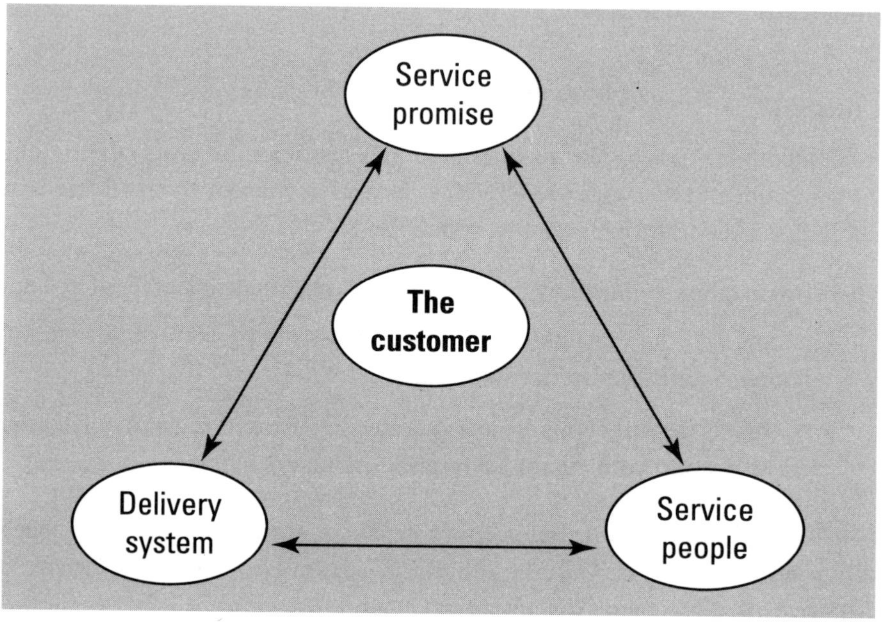

FIG 8.8: THE SERVICE TRIANGLE

In his book *Service America* Zemke proposes the above diagram to encapsulate the relationship between the four factors involved in the service.

We provide below the two checklists for:

- Promise (read Mission) – and for
- Delivery systems.

The checklist and a more full explanation of the model is to be found in Chapter 6, Service is a people business.

The service promise (mission) should:

- **Be a non-trivial statement of intent** – in as far as it really addresses the issues that are important to the firm's target group of customers.
- **Differentiate the service from its competition (i.e. a CDA[43])** – the organization becomes renowned for doing their thing better than the

rest – to the point that people talk about the firm ". . . . did you know that Nordstrom (the chain retailer) gives full refunds on damaged clothing even if its doubtful that it's their fault!" etc.

- **Have real economic and extrinsic value for the customers** – if your car is serviced at 'Windroute Autos', it not only means that it is safer, it's also more economic in that as a consequence it lasts longer, burns less fuel and runs further on the same set of tyres. But also, because they have a good reputation locally, dealing with them marks you out as someone who has good sense.
- **Be deliverable by the organization** – don't ever promise what the firm can't deliver. The key is to under promise and *over deliver*.

This promise/mission should provide the touchstone for decision-making within the organization. Any proposed changes to the way of working or the organization of the firm should be assessed for how well or otherwise this change will affect the firm's ability to deliver what it promises.

Communicating the promise, mainly internally, is as important as having it in the first place. This mission must be broadcast throughout the organization. It should be on the heading of all internal correspondence, it should be the catechism intoned at every team meeting, it should be the yardstick via which everything else in the organization is measured.

The delivery system should:

- **Be based on the service promise/mission** – it is the starting point for everything when in the 'process' delivery mode;
- **Be customer AND employee friendly** – if it's more convenient for the people in the back room who run the system (i.e. those who should serve, those who serve customers) the service delivery will fail to attain the service promise/mission.
- **Contain a 'feedback loop' for self correction** – this is where the MIS/CIS comes in play, and we see this in Chapter 13, Seriously seeking feedback.
- **Be invisible in normal operation** – the service loses its impact if the customers see how difficult it is to perform. Like all professionals, service must always appear easy. There was once an advertisement for some top of the range car, the advertisement featured a swan serenely gliding across a lake, during the shot the camera slipped

beneath the surface of the water and we were able to see that the said swan was paddling with great effort.

Early in the author's adolescent period of life – he had the privilege of working as a humble member of the caste for a few good restaurants -it was interesting to see the contrast of how calm and composed the really good waiters were (i.e. the ones who enjoyed the most tips) with the hell on earth that was going on in the kitchen on a good night. Yet the waiter had to deal with both appropriately, with the kitchen he had to be aggressively in pursuit of the needs of his tables, yet with the customers, serenity itself. The message: great things always appear easy no matter how much effort has gone into the production, the customer does not need to know.

- **Be provided.with adequate amounts of mission critical resources** – "For the want of a nail a horse was lost... " – and that lead to the loss of a kingdom. The principle applies even today. Whatever the goal, its achievement is ensured or otherwise by the degree to which adequate amounts of the 3 x Ms, i.e. Manpower, Material, and Money are provided. "Prior to the battle it was all strategy and tactics, but once the first shot had been fired, it was all logistics (General 'Storming Norman', Desert Storm 1992)" . . . . so is it the case in a service business.

  and finally:

- **The delivery system is to make the business profitable, not for the comfort of those who run the system!!**

Exercise

1. Identify where your service business is on the service specific Lovelock Matrices.
2. Determine what implications this has for your business, long and short-term.
3. Consider what stratagems Lovelock suggests for advantage, and how best you can employ these.

   Then, take a specific MoT episode and draw up a 'blueprint' of how this should proceed and be supported.

4. Finally, compare what it is you want to happen during the MoT above, and how well you think your business has developed all three aspects of the Service Triangle to enable this to come true.
   - What should your 'service promise' be?
   - What is required to ensure that your 'delivery system' is able to support the actions that your blueprint will require?

References

39 *As mentioned in the introduction, limited space in this book, and in the light of its full coverage elsewhere (see further reading at the end of the book) has forced us to omit the topic of 'Customer Service' per se.*

40 *We show a simple outline of a 'Blueprint' at the end of this chapter.*

41 *(J.O.K. Summer 1983 C.M. Lovelock 'Classifying Services to Gain Strategic Marketing Insights') and developed by McDonald in 'Marketing Planning Services', Adrian Payne 1996)*

42 *Education was there first via correspondence courses: The School of the Air in the Australian Outback and the Open University on television in the UK.*

43 *A Competitive Differential Advantage*

NINE

Managing service resources

NINE

Managing service resources

Introduction

"Before the battle it's all strategy and tactics, but once the enemy is engaged it's all logistics"

Norman Schwarzkopf – about 'managing' Desert Storm 1992

This chapter discusses the major issue that determines the quality of service delivered: the so called resource dilemma, or capacity constraint, and the various strategies and policies marketers of service products have evolved to cope with this important influence on their ability to provide excellent service profitably.

Resource dilemma – capacity constraint

The ability to provide the timely and efficient service process that will satisfy and delight the customer is critically constrained by the capacity of the resources available to the firm, and how they are managed.

Towards the end of the last chapter we saw that the service delivery system is a critical 'leg' of the Service Triangle, and the delivery system can only function to affect when it has adequate resources on-stream and at the right time.

The problem

As discussed prior, often the main part of the service product consists of the use of the firm's resource over time. This resource is frequently people but can also be hardware such as computer capacity, rolling stock, hotel beds, seats in the theatre et al, or some combination or permutation of these and more.

It is not just the quantity of this resource that constrains the capacity to deliver the service to the required standard but also (and in many cases mainly), the quality and reliability of this resource. Quality can deteriorate if the people providing the service are tired or over stressed. Old and/or ill-maintained equipment will let down the service deliverers usually when it matters most. *(This author's equivalent of Murphy's Law.)*

As we have just discussed in Chapter 8, successful marketing of the firm's service depends on a consistent quality of performance; it is **the main part** of the firm's marketing. However, the level of demand in any given marketplace will fluctuate over time, there will be more customers to be served at some times than at others. This cycle can be daily, take place over a week, over a year, be tied to some other phenomena such as the weather or appear to be totally unpredictable.

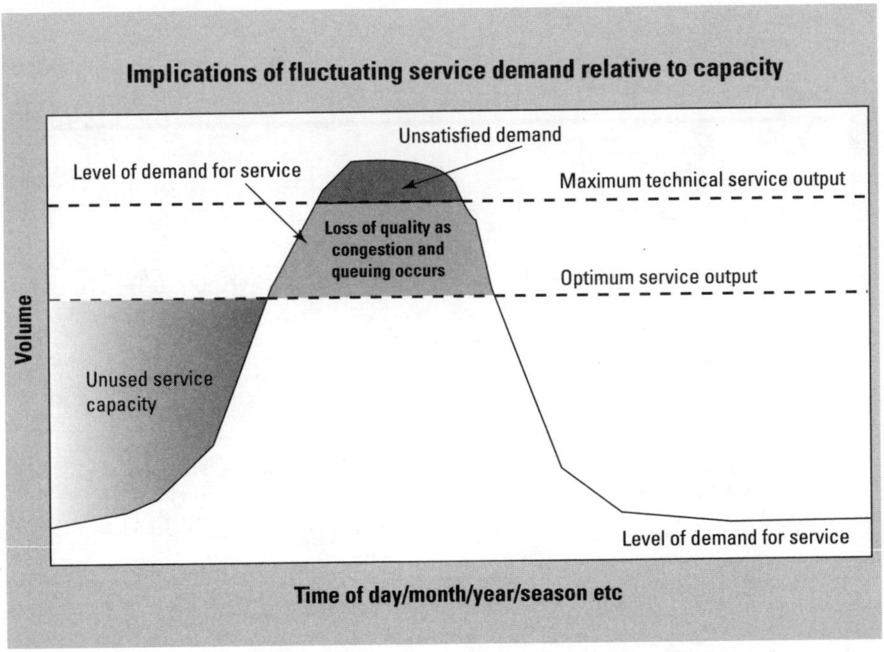

FIG 9.1: IMPLICATIONS OF FLUCTUATING SERVICE DEMAND RELATIVE TO CAPACITY

Consider Fig 9.1 above, the 80/20 Perato ratio (or something close) will frequently apply, in that for 80% of the time the market is slack, but for some 20% of the time it experiences peak demand. At peak times the key service resources come under more strain that it experiences at slack (normal) times.

Unless there are strategies to cope at times of peak demand, there is a greater probability that the quality of the service will suffer, than when the market is slack.

But whatever the circumstances, poor service delivery is the service marketer's problem, not the customer's.

If 'average demand' is greater than 80% of capacity, the firm is in trouble. Experience shows that in these cases the level of demand will too frequently be in excess of 'maximum technical output' causing untenable levels of customer dissatisfaction – leading to customer disaffection and revenge.

The service marketer must provide adequate resource/capacity to deliver their service to the customer, and yet at the same time ensure that the costs of doing so are reasonable and the firm can still make a profit.

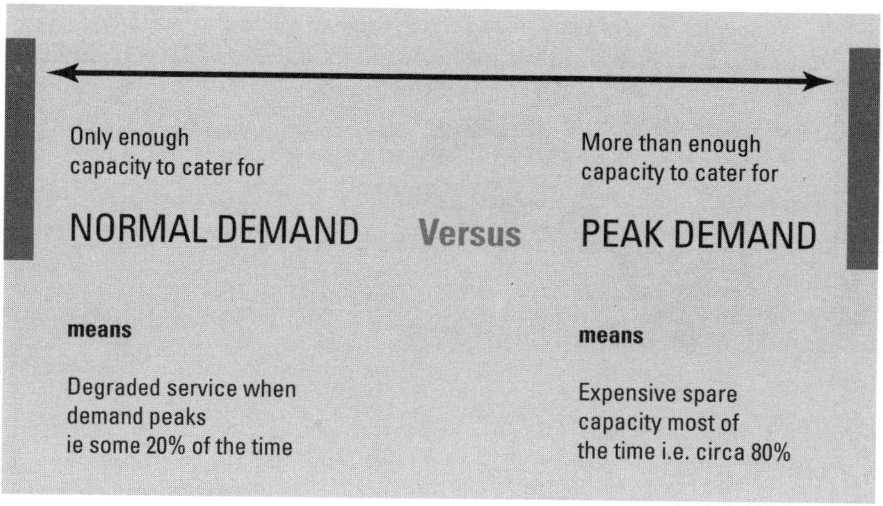

FIG 9.2: THE RESOURCE DILEMMA

Figure 9.2. encapsulates this vital issue, the service marketer must produce a strategy, which addresses this dilemma.

The right hand side of the diagram describes the sort of strategy adopted by engineers when designing bridges or North Sea oil rigs. These, when translated to the context of service, mean that the marketer provides more than enough resource capacity to satisfy the largest, reasonably foreseeable peak demand (and then some extra for safety). These resources are expensive – so unless the customer is unwilling, they must be passed on via higher prices. This happens occasionally, for example, at the top end of the hotel sector, or private health care.

However, this strategy is plainly uneconomic for most commercial companies. It will mean that a large portion of the firm's resource capacity will lie idle most of the time, particularly during periods of slack demand.

Resource capacity has a cost, even if only an opportunity cost, and during slack demand this spare capacity will not be generating revenue, so without some means of soaking up these 'idle' costs, the firm will bleed to death during periods of slack demand.

Thus, if resources are expensive, and/or cannot be laid off or redirected to other remunerative employment in slack periods, the temptation for most service sector firms is to provide just enough resource capacity (with very little margin) to satisfy 'normal' demand.

In some sectors, peaks may also bring in lower quality custom such as coach traffic to wayside hostelries in summer – these customers may yield a short-term increase in profits – but long-term they will drive valuable regular customers away.

The left hand end of the continuum is beloved by the accounts department who wish to screw down the costs of any operation (and often rightly so).

This left hand option will inevitably result in a poorer quality 'process' when the market peaks, unless some strategy to compensate is employed.

The hope is that in the face of his poor service delivery, either the customer, who represents the valuable core business, will stoically tolerate the inconvenience, or that those customers who do leave as a result can easily be replaced.[44]

The table below sets out some frequent areas of conflict that must be addressed by the service marketer when trying to resolve the need to delight customers, whilst also keeping costs under control.

Neither of the two extremes of the continuum as per Fig 9.2 above are satisfactory, so the successful service marketer is the one who resorts to creating innovative strategies to bridge the demands of the two goals, i.e. delighting customers and doing so efficiently.

The conflicting issues

To be resolved when addressing the 'resource dilemma'

PROCESS ISSUES	OPERATIONS ISSUES	MARKETING AIMS & CONCERNS
The management capacity	Cap costs by reducing underutilization of resource	Service availability and quality can be compromised in demand peaks
Management of customer queues	Optimize the use of available resource by planning and maintaining customer order and discipline	Firm must not be seen by customers as being unresponsive
The design of service delivery tasks	Reduce error, waste and fraud exploit technology for efficiencies, simplify via standardization	The firm can be seen as unresponsive if service deliverers are too
Layout and design of the service facilities	Improve cost effectiveness and enhance safety and security	Customers must not be confused nor must find the facilities unattractive

FIG 9.3: THE RESOURCE DILEMMA (II)

Coping with resource dilemma

When in-house capacity is enough to cope with the highest probable peaks in demand – the firm can consider…

'PRICING TO PAY FOR 'DOWN-TIME'. Although this is the more unusual of the two extremes, this is the more successful precedent. This policy is possible IF, and only IF, the firm's competitive position[45] is strong enough. Prices should be high enough to ensure sufficient profit to carry the costs of surplus resource in slack times.

Apart from top-end hotels and private hospitals – other examples of where this can be done is top-end firms in auditing, and in consultancy.

Some of the large auditing partnerships and consultancies employ a strategy that combines the above premium price position with a very low cost of operation. This low cost is achieved mainly by paying comparatively low wages to their graduate trainees (who do most of the 'heavy' productive work during peak auditing periods).

These firms compensate for low wages by providing very attractive training packages for their graduate trainees. This training takes place during slack times. The quality of the training given, plus the kudos of having such a high status firm on the trainees' résumé, ensures that there is always a large queue of new graduates waiting to join.

In return, when the workload peaks it is 'all hands to the pump' for (almost) 24 hour/seven day weeks.

Other service businesses use a premium price policy to reduce overall fee carrying workload and employ the hiatus for study, authorship, personal development (training) and networking. If they price too 'competitively' their offering soon becomes stale – and all too soon **that is all they can charge.**

PRICE AS A 'SHEPHERD'

In the context of price and resource, it is common in the service sector for firms to have a pricing policy which differentiates the service according to where it is consumed in the business demand cycle. The aim of such a pricing policy is to move demand from the peaks to the 'troughs'. Thus the railways will charge more for traveling during rush hours. Airlines will do something similar for peak times of day, and days of the year. Tour package operators and other holiday providers will charge more for their services at the height of the season etc.

Between the two extremes of the capacity continuum the situation is that firms will have a certain amount of spare capacity until demand starts to surge. The more the firm's resource capacity is located toward the right of the continuum (as in Fig 9.2 above), the more of this capacity they will have lying idle and soaking up profit during normal demand.

The principle strategy to handle this situation is to use any spare capacity for other money earning purposes until required by the main business.

An example of this is the way that a particular market research agency ensures access to sufficient office resource when it needs it, yet avoids bleeding to death when it does not. Most of the time in the market research business there is need for only a modest amount of administrative resource. However, from the moment that a project's fieldwork is completed, in the rush to meet the report deadline for the client, the research agency will go into overdrive with a voracious appetite for office resource. The need is for 'round-the-clock', 'seven-days-a-week' access, which means that this resource cannot be outsourced, access must be guaranteed as and when required.

The research agency in mind has therefore set-up its administrative facility as an office services bureau offering book-keeping, word processing and desk top publishing to local businesses, colleges and universities.

The agency accepts work for the bureau only if it has long or loose deadlines, and in return it charges very low prices. This way such work can be set aside when the more profitable market research requires attention. The low price is possible because the aim is only to cover the wages of the administrative staff involved in the office services work and the variable costs.

Other less extreme examples of the strategy of using capacity for other revenue earning work in slack times are:

- Computer catastrophe back up[46], where the computer bureau providing the service will sell low cost 'block time' on the mainframe when not required by the back-up clients.
- Hotel special event weekends, such as 'Agatha Christie Weekends' where they play the game of 'Who Murdered the Manager'. Or low cost breaks where the accommodation may even be free and the customers only pay for the meals consumed. These, and other attractions, are ways in which the normally spare capacity at weekends can earn some contribution rather than lie idle.

- Airlines using their scheduled route aircraft for holiday charter at times of the year when the business traffic is slack, etc.

However, this strategy gets increasingly difficult to apply as the firm moves towards the intellectual property end of the Service Spectrum. What can a solicitor do in slack times – wait table? Engage in landscape gardening? Run a window cleaning business? Or what?

'Providing only enough capacity to satisfy normal demand'

As a result of recession, many, if not most, firms will downsize to this point, (i.e. not even enough resource for slack times) and many are loath to take on more capacity subsequently, preferring to out-source even for normal requirements, sometimes to the extent of out-placing this part of the business to other English speaking parts of the world such as India.

At this end of the continuum, in order to successfully delight customers, the service marketer must create a strategy that brings extra capacity on-line as and when required, and to the right quality.

This appears simple to do via one or a combination of such policies as:

- subcontracting excess demand,
- 'body shopping' (i.e. staffing-up for the duration of the peak),
- part-time and/or flexi-time workers.

But each of the above has a strong potential to generate undesirable outcomes for the firm, mainly by lowering the quality of experience for the customer when served by the firm at other than 'slack' times.

For example, there is a high probability that workers who are 'body shopped' will not have the same level of training, motivation and commitment as the rest of the permanent team. This inevitably leads to a lowering of process quality.

This deficiency also frequently applies to part-time and casual workers, especially if the firm has no commitment to them.

Understandably these people will often have a 'casual' attitude. It appears not to matter how hard they work; soon they will have to look for yet another job when this one finishes.

A similar situation can apply to sub-contractors: they will not have the same level and content of training or experience, and unless action is taken to address this, they will have different standards.

In addition there is always the danger that the sub-contractor will 'back door' the firm. This is where the client and the sub-contractor will cut-out the principal firm and go direct to each other next time thus saving cost and shortening communications for themselves.

The danger of being 'back door-ed' increases the more the business is located toward the intellectual property end of the Service Spectrum.

However, the problems identified above are not invariably the case, in some industries such as graphic design, audio publications, and to an extent market research, the culture strongly inhibits such behavior. So much work is channeled through the principal firms, i.e. those issuing the sub-contracts, that it would be commercial suicide to even try to cut them out.

A possible strategy to avoid being back door-ed is for the principle to become a well-known source of good profitable work for sub-contractors. This suits a market where the balance of supply and demand is in favour (i.e. there are more firms looking for work than there is work available).

There are proven ways to ameliorate the downside inherent to the strategies of body shopping, or providing part-time/flexi-time work. The principle is to gain the commitment of the people who are used by the firm to provide the required extra capacity. The way to do this is to provide some benefits in addition to the wage for the job. The most successful benefits tend to be:

- Training that improves the worker's market value,

  and/or

- Retainers,

  and/or

- Guarantees of more work where that came from.

Two examples of being a source of work and training are worth citing:

The first example relates to the horse racing industry.

A typical racecourse will only host meetings (i.e. run horse races) for a very few days per year. So for most of the year, for essential administration and maintenance etc. a racecourse will employ at most only a half a dozen people full-time, whilst for meetings they will outsource many more.

During a race meeting the racecourse will be required to provide race goers (i.e. customers) with food and drink, car parking, on-course betting etc. The course will also need security, cleaning services etc. There is no way that a racecourse can afford to employ these facilities full-time when they will only be generating income for such a small part of the year.

Catering services and on-course betting are sub-contracted[47] as is security and sometimes even car parking.

However, during the meeting (which lasts from two to five days), the provision of car park attendants and cleaning and ground repair between the ravages of each race day, will have to be obtained by the racecourse hiring people directly for the duration of that meeting. Even though these are relatively humble tasks, the people performing them will frequently come into contact with the race going customers. Thus, it is important that they perform their tasks to the standard required, *and* that their interpersonal behaviors should complement the race day experience (i.e.'process') for the customer.

To ensure access to the right quality of people, it has been known for a group of racecourses to come together to create an informal syndicate. The syndicate will arrange that there will be few days, if any, when any two of the syndicate will hold meetings on the same day. Between members they recruit a small corps of occasional/part-time workers who will be used by each course in turn to provide these non-sub-contracted tasks on race days.

These workers are guaranteed a certain number of day's employment per year. They are provided with work-wear and training to the necessary standards. The syndicate provides race day transport. Individuals are collected from home and taken to the course by minibus early on race days and returned the same way that evening.

The workers benefit from:

- A guaranteed number of days work per year,
- Work-wear, not wearing out their own clothes,

- Training in a whole range of saleable skills,
- The possible referral of more work in the syndicate whenever it crops up.

The syndicate gains from having access to a motivated and reliable workforce during race days at a reasonable cost.

The second example is an approach to providing extra capacity at 'special times'. Several airlines in the USA have provided a method of staff coverage for the eventuality of bad weather, which often, but unpredictably occurs in the 'Mid West'. When a storm hits they will often require emergency staffing levels at those airports that are effected by bad weather (usually heavy snow storms, or freezing rain episodes in the winter months).

The practice is to 'retain' former employees of the airline, who act as 'reservists' and who agree to hold themselves in readiness on a rota, to be called in to help when required. A practice, which is similar to the English, small town, part-time fireman system.

A note of caution for lean or 'flat' organizations is to obtain the healthy internal criticism any business needs in order to prevent becoming stultified by complacency.

Any firm that wishes to address the 'resource dilemma' via a strategy of being a 'flat' organization, (perhaps also organized around 'self directed teams', and 'out-sourcing' extra capacity when required at peak times), must be aware that outside suppliers do not normally have the same willingness to criticize and improve their clients as do (secure) employees.

Few outsiders will dare say the unsay-able, as to do so could put their livelihood at risk. Thus a lean and 'flat' type of organization brings with it the danger that the firm will not have the benefit of the internal early warning signals, or the outlandish new idea that could put it ahead of the competition. It will not be until the market communicates its displeasure (usually in the form of a disappearing customer base) that anything will appear amiss. By the time this is noticed dramatic damage to the business may have already been done, and it may be too late to effect repair.

An example of this happening was the near demise of the training arm of a major UK professional body (even its chartered status gave no protection). In the '80s, the institution ran a very profitable professional training operation for members and non-members alike. This was conducted at home and abroad.

The job of the institute was to provide the training facilities (including hotel style accommodation for public courses) and database promotion, whilst expensive freelance trainers were used to deliver the courses.

We can see here the insight of the original founders making part of the operation a variable cost as part of their strategy for handling the resource dilemma.

Towards the end of the '80s most of the training faculty were well aware of the danger signals on the horizon. However, as outside suppliers, it was important to stay 'in the good books' of those who hired or fired them, so most said nothing because they knew the tendency of indigenous management is to ignore bad news, especially when coming from those outside the organization (the mentality being to treat them as non team members).

In the early '90s the indigenous management team underwent great changes and the new team of managers, like all new brooms decided to make a clean sweep *without* the understanding of the original founders of the training arm.

Result: by the end of the '90s the facilities had become almost a ghost town for most of the time. This trend was accelerated by a change in the balance of courses from open public courses which brought in profitable business for the hotel facilities owned by the organization, to client specific courses which were not only less profitable, charging by the trainer day as opposed to the participant day, but were making no contribution whatsoever towards the fixed costs of the accommodation facilities.

Make sure this does not happen to you!!

Exercise

A. Review your industry over the last two years or so – look for patterns of customer usage and the fluctuating customer demand that provoked this peak or that trough.

What sort of cycle regularly occurs:

i Usage (e.g. public transport for commuting) is it:

- Daily
- Weekly
- Monthly
- Seasonal?

Or

ii Some combination of these?

B. Does this pattern of demand/usage cause your business to have either:

iii Frenetic times with:

- Not enough capacity to cope,
- Many customers either getting poor service, or no service at all,
- Customers not coming back when demand slackens and capacity is no longer under strain?

Or

iv Very quiet times where your business may have expensive capacity lying idle?

C. Over a recent typical year,[48] (say) what is your average load factor (i.e. volume of usage divided by your volume capacity at full stretch)?

NB if this 'load factor' is much greater than 80% over a full business cycle, the quality of the service experience for your customers is indubitably suffering.

If your analysis of 'A' & 'B' above shows your firm is often stretched, and 'C' that your average load factor is well above 80% – there is a need for some firm managerial action – what action do you intend to take – raise prices to reduce demand? Use 'shepherd pricing' (see Chapter 12, Pricing a service business) to control when demand occurs AND/OR add capacity, if so how will you do this as economically as possible?

If – on the other hand – your analysis indicates no such problems, indeed your average load factor is well under 80%, do you think you are over resourced, or over priced?

Is there merit in considering that you adopt some combination of reducing capacity (thus saving costs) and/or reducing price (thus increasing revenue)?

References

44 *This of course neglects the damage done to the business by the 'disappointed advocates'*

45 *Such as is enjoyed by the monopolies of the Post Office, or Water Boards.*

46 *Sometimes referred to as 'Disaster Recovery'.*

47 *Because the subcontractors are buying access to an audience for their business, the more that the audience of race goers who attend the meeting are attractive customers, then the greater the numbers of these sub-contractors will the racecourse have to choose from, and the better the deal that course managers will be able to obtain from these service providers.*

48 *If there is no typical year, then take the arithmetic mean of the last five years.*

TEN

Segmenting a service market

TEN

Segmenting a service market

Introduction

"When you are not as big as your opponent – you have to be more clever"

Michael Collins (The Big Fella)

This chapter discusses:

- Why and how a market can be segmented for a service product
  - the pre-conditions necessary,
  - the classes of segment that can be created,
  - the sequence in which a segment should be built, and
  - it illustrates this topic with some examples of successful segmentation in the service sector.

The chapter then proceeds to discuss:

- time, the only objective dimension on which a service product can be segmented, the constraints this entails and the five 'flavours' in which it should be considered and the opportunities that open up thereby[49].

Segmentation: Why do it?

The need for 'focus'

Segmentation is based on the premise that *'Marketing is a dialogue over time with a **specific group of customers** whose needs the marketer gets to understand in depth. etc.' (Professor McDonald – as per Chapter 1).*

This in turn is based on the key 'strategic imperative', of '**focus**', which states that:

> *'The more an enterprise focuses its attentions, resource and effort on a specific goal, the greater the probability of success. The more any effort is diluted across many activities the less will be the probabilities of success.'*[50]

This imperative is accentuated by the fact that 'market share' is a precursor of market power. The firm with the largest market share can become the 'price maker' (i.e. it sets the market price which is the maximum that direct competitors can charge, any more and their customers will go elsewhere). The smaller the market share, the greater the chance that the firm is a 'price taker' (i.e. one third of the profit equation, [Price x Volume = Revenue, and Revenue – Cost = Profit], is now out of the firm's direct control, a lower price may mean increasing volume, but this will rarely equate to an increased profit).

This in turn reflects the strategic imperative of 'Never engaging an opponent on ground of their own choosing', 'Never take them head-on', unless that is, you can afford a war of attrition in that you have overwhelming superiority of whatever resource it takes, money, people, talent etc. To do otherwise is a sure recipe for disaster.

Segmentation is the 'flank attack', applied to marketing[51], via exploiting the benefits of 'focus'; it enables the marketer to avoid direct confrontation with competitors.

Segmentation creates opportunities for the smaller firm, offering ways into the larger market, and because of this it is a tremendous potential threat for the larger incumbent. Via segmentation new entrants can nibble away at the market leader's business – UNLESS the larger firm has anticipated this eventuality with pre-emptive preventative measures, but this is easier said than done. The only viable preventative action that can be taken in commerce (as opposed to real politics, or war, which is only 'politics by other means') is to pre-segment the market, to get so close to the customers that the opponent will have to fight on the pre-segmenter's terms. That is to say, the assailant will have to attack the incumbent 'head-on', on the ground which they will have prepared for the fight, what the military refer to as the 'Killing Ground'.

To reprise: segmentation is the division of the general market into smaller sub markets (McDonald's 'Specific Groups of Customers') so that the firm can get closer to the customer than otherwise would be the case.

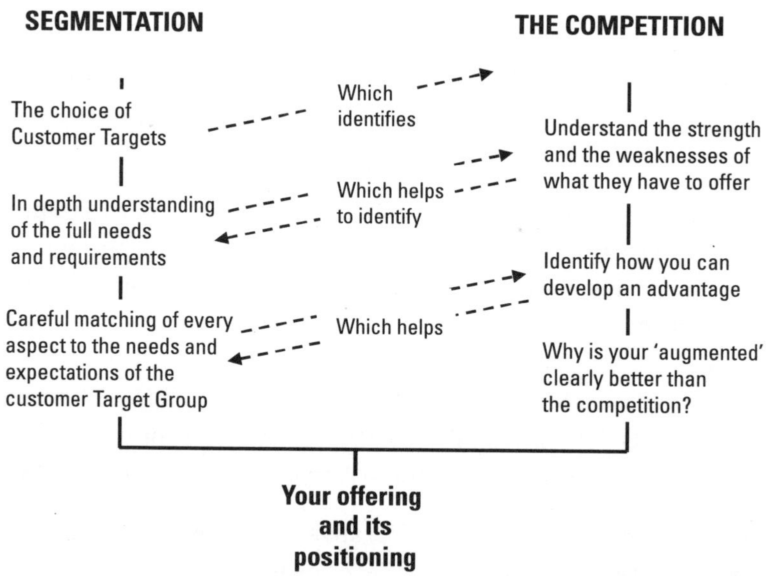

FIG 10.1: THE POSITIONING PROCESS

The characteristics of a viable segment are that:

- customers within the segment have more in common with each other in terms of their needs re. the service product, than they have with those customers/prospects outside the segment[52]
- in the perception of the customers/prospects in the segment, the firm more closely addresses their needs, than do any competitors.

Please note: *addressing a given segment requires a discrete marketing mix, not just the adaptation of the service product and/or promotion. For any segmentation to succeed, each element of the whole mix must be tailored* *specifically so that the mix addresses the needs and behaviors of the prospects in that segment.*

Pre-conditions for segmentation

Three conditions must be present in the market so as to establish a segment. There must be:

1. a gap in the market,
2. a market in the gap, and
3. the gap/market must be accessible to the marketer.

To expand:

A GAP IN THE MARKET exists if customers either believe they have needs which are not being specifically and currently satisfied by competitors already in the market, or they can be persuaded that this is the case.

A MARKET IN THE GAP exists if the amount of business that can be obtained from these prospects/customers is actually or potentially profitable enough to warrant the necessary investment.

It is this aspect that provides the greatest opportunity to the smaller firm and the greatest threat for the larger incumbent. Smaller firms will usually have the greater flexibility and lower overhead costs that will enable them to exploit relatively small segments (niches). Whereas the larger players will not only find it difficult to address the variety of needs in smaller segments, the size of their overheads will erode any potential profitability therein.

An example of this is the viability of Saga Holidays (i.e. vacations for the over 50's) in the face of the might of the major multinational tour operators.

The niche for a holiday catering to the experience and tastes of the over 50s who are either retired or about to was initially thought to be too small and specialist to be a profitable market for the likes of (say) Thompsons or Air Tours (not counting the fact that people of mature age would prefer not to share their leisure time with the 'sun, sand, sea and sex brigade', which does not typify all package holidays but it is the images 'Saga louts' often have of them).

The danger to the large incumbent firm is that the smaller player will conduct the commercial equivalent of guerrilla warfare, sometimes called rolling segmentation. Here the invader will 'cherry pick' (a strategy whereby the firm will address the high value but small volume parts of the market). In the initial stages the non-astute incumbent rarely sees the threat, indeed may even consider that the invader is doing them a favor by satisfying what are perceived to be a small, hard-to-please group of awkward and often demanding customers.

The 'invader' will collect a series of 'cherries'. No 'cherry' will be allowed to get to the size that it can become a market in the gap for the incumbent. Usually the incumbent wakes up to the threat when it dawns on them that they are being left with only the low value, high volume business.

By then it's too late. At this stage any attack on any of the invader's 'cherries' will be unopposed, the invader will not stand and fight, they will just fade into the night, and whilst the incumbent is consolidating their reclaimed customers, (at enormous cost to them) the invader will be picking another 'cherry' elsewhere.

A MARKET IS ACCESSIBLE if the marketer can:

- communicate with it by way of research, marketing information **and** promotion, and
- deliver/distribute the service to the customers, appropriately.

No matter how attractive a segment appears to be, if it is inaccessible to the service marketer, it may as well not exist. There are many factors which can make a segment inaccessible they range from:

- the inability to differentiate between the segment prospects and the rest of the market; for example, there may be no characteristic or behavior that discriminates a prospect in one segment from one who is not. Outwardly they are no different from the rest; they do not buy, use or consume the service product any differently.

To where:

- promotion to one segment can contaminate the firm's position in another, particularly where one of the segments is the 'main market', i.e. it accounts for the largest portion of profit.

This problem usually arises when there is some inter-segment alienation.

For example:

- in business to business markets: one segment is 'Greenpeace' the other is the 'Defense Industry', or one firm is in Israel, the other in Saudi Arabia;
- in consumer markets: one segment is a different race to the other.

Classes of segment

The trend nowadays is for the service marketer to countenance smaller and smaller segments so as to get closer and closer to the prospects/customers than the opposition.

> **The closer they can get to a customer, the more certain they are of 'locking out' the competitors.**

It will be helpful briefly to discuss the varying sizes of segment and their uses. The author knows of no accepted useful definitions of the following types of segment, even the latest *Marketing Dictionary*[53] is deficient in this matter.

It can be misleading to try and size a segment in absolute terms such as volume or value, or numbers of customers. What would be a large segment in one market would be insignificant in another. Thus because the size of any segment can only be relative to the size of the overall market from which it may be drawn, any possible measure would have to be either as a fraction or a percentage of that overall market and the author knows of no consensus on this matter. However, the following is offered for consideration, on the basis that it has proved helpful in the author's career as a Director of two very successful companies and a Managing Director of his own Marketing Research Agency.

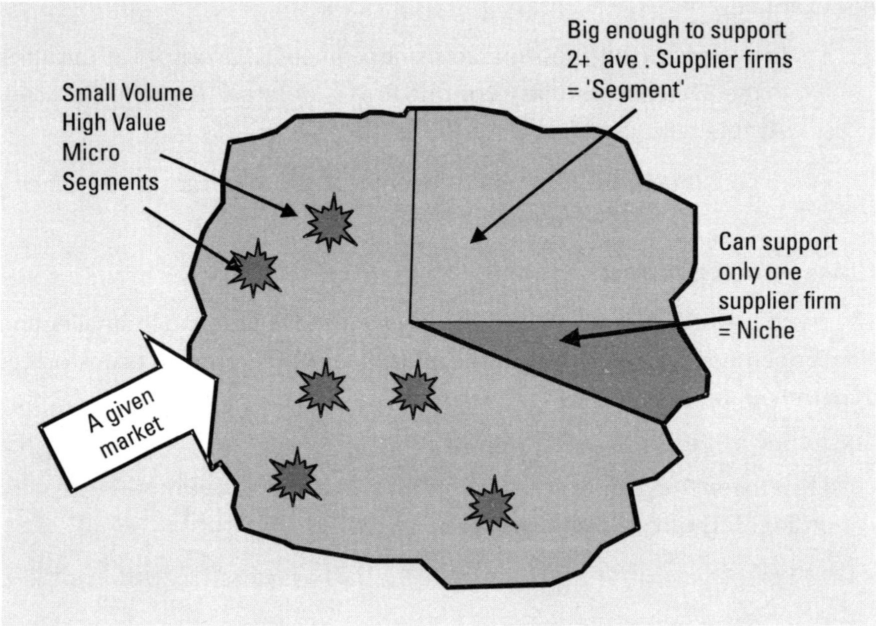

FIG 10.2: CLASSES OF SEGMENT

SEGMENT – in addition to being the generic name, it should be considered to be a group of customers that make up enough business to be capable of supporting two or more averaged size firms in the market.

NICHE – a small segment, more specialist than its larger cousin, and only capable of supporting one average size firm.

CHERRY – the main characteristic distinguishing a 'cherry' is its comparatively high value to volume ratio. Nominally circa <1.05% of the parent market or less, frequently within the ones and twos percentiles, and often smaller than this.

For survival, any firm, that is only in this market, will either be very small[54] to survive on one 'cherry'[55] or that firm's business will be spread over several 'cherries'.

As discussed above, the purpose of this approach is to filter out the lower value business, usually from a mature, or maturing market.

A micro segment/cherry would be used by a new entrant to gain a bridgehead in a market dominated by otherwise well entrenched offerings from the main players.

This is a favorite strategy of the smaller firm when entering a market new to them. It was used to great effect by Direct Line (they of the red, musical telephone) when building their business in their early days. Direct Line would only target postcodes of known low risk lifestyle and 'up market' demographic profiles – potential business from outside their target group was rejected.

Direct Line is still effectively a niche player, as are Virgin Direct.

MICRO MARKETS/CHERRIES – are a genre in their own right. A micro market is an extremely small segment in terms of the absolute numbers of customers addressed:

- **In business-to-business markets**, micro markets can contain as few as one customer each, this is known as a 'Key Account' strategy.
- **In consumer markets**, referred to as 'salami-slices' (mainly by American's) which can involve segments consisting of as few as ten customers.

An illustration of this is the use of loyalty cards:

Over and above being a phenomenally rich source of information about buyer behavior, the ultimate purpose of the various loyalty card schemes is to 'salami-slice' their markets, to get as close to us as the better local corner grocer did in days gone by.

PLEASE NOTE

Throughout the rest of this book, particularly this chapter, unless specifically referring to one of the above types, the generic term 'segment' will be used.

General approach – the method

The service marketer will segment their market via the route described by the diagram Fig. 10.3 below. Starting at the left hand in search of unfulfilled prospect or customer needs, then, trying to discern how these needs are associated with customer characteristics. That is to say, "what benefits do prospects want, and which prospects want them?".

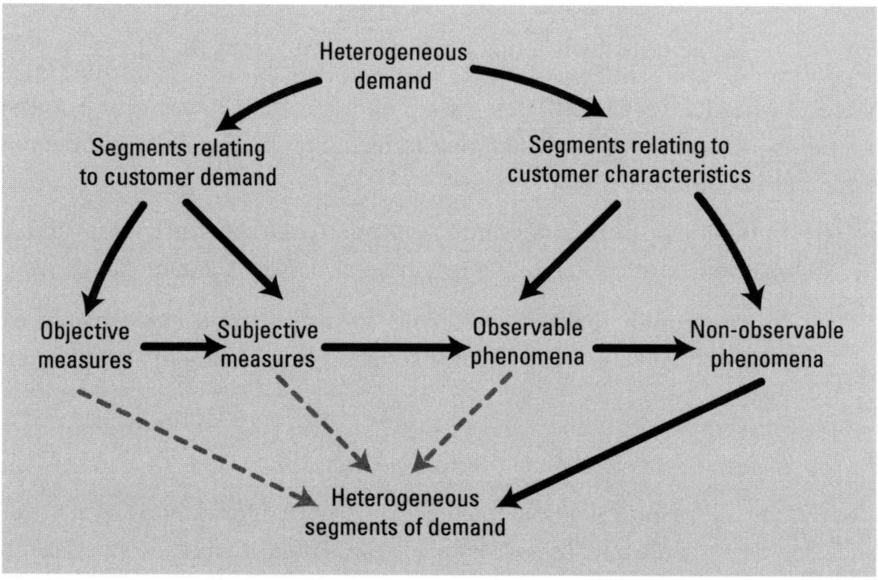

FIG 10.3: SIMPLIFIED CLASSIFICATION OF SEGMENTATION STRATEGIES

First – identify the benefits/competitive advantage

In searching for unsatisfied needs, the service marketer will first identify what needs should be addressed by what benefits in order to obtain a competitive advantage in this segment. These desired benefits can be categorized as 'Objective' and 'Subjective' measures.

When the product is a service, there is only one source of objective benefits, and that is 'Time'. (We examine this later in this chapter).

Therefore the service marketer must do everything to take advantage of the very subjective nature of a service which means that, with skill, the identical 'generic' ('core') and 'expected' parts of the product can, to all intents, be identical from one segment to another. To differentiate, it may only be necessary to address the 'augmented' part of the product (see Chapter 5).

Thus, in addition to time, the service marketer will draw on the extended mix, mainly people, process, physical evidence and resource.

FOR PEOPLE the service marketer could segment with the use of:

1. Inter-customer homogeneity – i.e. choosing customers that would get on well together. The various enclosures at a racecourse illustrate:
   - The Royal Enclosure at Ascot for the aristocrats,
   - Member's Enclosure for the better off,
   - Silver Ring for the middle classes, and
   - Tattersals (where the bookies congregate) for the remainder.

2. Similarly the market could be segmented in terms of the harmony between customers and staff – and where there could be disharmony because of the clash of lifestyles of those employed versus that of the clients' intermediaries – who will better 'chime' with the client. A good example of this happening is the young mega-brain eccentric techies who write software and the blue suits that buy the software being buffered by suitable account executives.

FOR PROCESS the service marketer would examine the market for needs such as:

3. Status – and the process of serving the customer could address this by doing everything to confer status on the customer (see the example of Business First and airline travel following). Status is often associated with the appropriate physical evidence (for example, the bride's Rolls Royce at a wedding or the top table for important guests at functions).

4. To be fussed over, i.e. made to feel cared for (which is allied to – but not the same as status) so the process would be designed to confer the impression that 'nothing is too much trouble' for the customer. Examples of this being the use of beauticians, bespoke tailors and personal trainers.

5. For the service to be perceived as efficient – minimum fuss, maximum punctuality.

RESOURCE

6. Here the market can be segmented to differentiate between those customers who must be served at peak times (therefore will pay more) and those who are more flexible as to when they are served (and therefore can be persuaded via 'shepherding' prices to move their concentration from peak demand on to the shoulder).

Two extreme examples of this to illustrate:

- **Healthcare:** Private vs. NHS segments.
- **And air travel:** First or Business Class vs. Coach.

Medical health care[56]

The core part of this range of products is as close to being identical as medical ethics can obtain. The products, (private vs. NHS) start to diverge at the expected, with such issues as the manner in which the consultant will deal with the patient. In the private segment, service is friendlier and patients can jump the queue, at least for the initial appointment. Plus more time is given to the patient (i.e. it is less hurried) and if appropriate, the consultant will visit every day.

The augmented part of the health care product is what mostly differentiates it:

PROCESS

Time is used as an objective benefit via shorter waiting lists, quicker processing of admission and other admin. In addition, some subjective benefit via more attentive hospital staff, a generally 'warmer' (vs. NHS) personal attitude from the staff and medical teams to the patient/customer.

PEOPLE

More staff per patient, more motivation because of the way the firm is perceived to value them, which, with more pleasant working conditions, produces a propensity toward more customer care.

PHYSICAL EVIDENCE

Higher specification of all the tangibles, such as the waiting rooms, reception area, patients' bedrooms, the food service, general furniture etc. the list goes on and on.

Airline First and Business Classes

The main problem for the airlines is that they must justify the premium rates they charge for First and Business Classes but the Generic and the Expected are identical and a great deal of that is to do with Time. The back and the front of the plane (hopefully) both take off and land at the same instant.

On most airlines the order in which luggage appears on the conveyor often depends on the class in which the passenger was traveling. On some airlines First Class luggage goes straight to the passenger's hotel room, where applicable.

So the airline will address the 'subjective' aspects to differentiate one segment from another.

PROCESS

Time is used wherever possible. First and Business Classes are given fast-track check-in and boarding, are allowed to get on and leave the plane first. Those traveling in the back of the plane, coach and economy are deliberately (and on some airlines ostentatiously) prevented from disembarking until those in the front of the plane have left.

Those in First and Business who do board early can often enjoy the superiority of enjoying their complimentary drink whilst the hoi polloi traveling in the back file by on their way to their seats.

During the flight, meals and drinks are first served to the First and Business Classes and frequently faster than they are served to those in the back.

The limousine service now so prevalent combines:

- 'Process' (personal attention and convenience)
- with time (less waiting around, less hassle accessing long-term car parking)
- and cost (long-term car parking isn't cheap).

PEOPLE

The service given to passengers who travel at the front of the plane is faster and more attentive due to the higher ratio of airline personnel to passengers, both on the ground, and in the air.

PHYSICAL EVIDENCE

Most airlines will have special lounges and other facilities in which passengers at the front of the plane can await departure. Several now also have VIP lounges and Business Class facilities at ports of arrival.

At the front of the plane, seats are wider and more luxurious both in terms of comfort, seat pitch (space between rows) and degrees of recline, compared to the back. Video monitor screens are larger and on some airlines there is even a greater choice of entertainment. There are also usually more toilets per passenger for those who have paid more for their ticket.

The list goes on and will continue to grow with the increasing competition for these higher paying segments.

Not only is the airline industry suffering from over capacity, but also more firms, particularly in Europe, are cutting back on the amount of Business Class travel they will pay for. It is not uncommon for firms to stipulate that their managers should travel by coach for all journeys of three hours or less. At the time of writing, nearly half of all European firms whose managers have to travel by air, have such a policy; indeed some 46% of German firms stipulate coach for all personnel other than the most senior.[57] Currently we are also witnessing, throughout the world, a dramatic rise in the fortunes of the budget airlines such as SouthWestern in the USA, Ryan Air and Easy Jet in Europe, and Virgin Blue and Air Asia in South East Asia.

Next – discover who are the prospects that want these benefits

Referring back to Fig 10.3, the service marketer must now find ways to access the prospects that make up his/her potential segment. They will now examine the factors on the right hand routes to segmentation in that diagram, i.e. the segments re. customer characteristics.

OBSERVABLE PHENOMENA – are the physical attributes that people or businesses have, and/or those buying behaviors they manifest, which can be recognized and described by a reasonably intelligent, though not necessarily intensively trained observer.

Often these phenomena are relatively unsophisticated, e.g. for consumer markets, such attributes as: the standard demographics:

- Age
- Gender
- Class (i.e. blue vs. white-collar workers)
- Race etc.

For business to business markets, such attributes as:

- Company size,
- Standard Industrial Classification (SIC code),
- How long established,
- Location, etc.

For both business and consumer, buying behaviors such as:

- Buy-type,
- New task,
- Modified re-buy,
- Routine response or straight re-buys

Buy Phase,

- Problem recognition, to
- Search routines, to
- Post use review

i.e. Where do they buy? How do they buy? Who do they refer to for advice? What is the search behavior, by whom and how is it conducted etc?

NON-OBSERVABLE PHENOMENA – this requires a skilled approach for which the person doing the classification should be especially trained.

Its main application is in consumer markets and the phenomena in question are to do with personality, psychographics[58] and lifestyle.[59]

Much of the 'non-observable' is brought together in what is known as 'geo-demographic' segmentation methods which link the above with demographics, and with habitation (put simply – 'where they live').

In the UK there are several providers of this most powerful tool, amongst which are:

- CACI with their product = ACORN* *(*A Classification of Residential Neighbourhood),*
- PinPoint = main propriety product being FinPin, for financial services,

And

- Mosaic = similar to ACORN but approached in a unique way.

Each of the above is a very powerful segmentation tool for consumer markets. They are based on the expression of the human preference to live in neighbourhoods where we feel comfortable with our neighbours. (i.e. birds of a feather, flock together).

The principle of how these tools are generated is to analyze the correlation of the associated buyer behaviors with the location where the people with these behaviors live. The statistical link in the United Kingdom[60] is via a 'Cluster Analysis' of the data against the enumeration districts of the National Census. These districts are described in relation to the National Grid, as are postcodes/zip codes etc.

There is also a great deal of published 'continuous market/ing research' which is cross-analyzed by geo-demographics (such as Mintel, TGI etc.).

Thus, if a service marketer has the postcodes of their current customers, they can tell what lifestyles they are addressing (how best to position the service product and what else they may be interested in).

The tool's proprietors will also be able to identify where to find other potential customers, like those already served by the firm, so that the marketer can know where to go so as to get more of the same. This last must be the first consideration because this strategy (with the inelegant name of 'feeding the pig') is the least costly way of growing a consumer business.

The various proprietors can also supply databases of names and addresses to help access these new prospects.

The facilities provided, and the scope of these tools, are constantly being developed so that even though the tools are more than three decades old at the time of writing, service marketers have only just started to scratch the surface of the potential for geo-demographics in consumer markets.

The reader should contact each proprietor to discover, in depth, what is available for him or her.

Putting the segmentation strategy together

The first caution at this stage is to take care. If it is at all possible, do not segment the market on the same basis as the competition:

- They will not have the same perspective as you;
- They may not have got it right.

Exercise

1. How does your firm segment its current customer base?
2. How do you intend to improve this aspect of the marketing of your business?

References

49 *For a discussion of the basics of segmentation, the reader is referred to the author's book 'Mastering Marketing'- Chapter 3.*

50 *This is a tricky balancing act for the marketer, especially where the product is a service. Too much 'Focus', as cited in the cases of railways, or the film industry (in the seminal HBR paper 'Marketing Myopia' by Theodore Levitt), can mean that threats and opportunities are not spotted in time, the nose is "too close to the grindstone". The Service Marketer has to focus sufficiently on the tasks in hand, whilst keeping a good 'lookout' for developments in his/her business environment.*

51 *'Marketing Warfare', Ries & Trout.*

Continued over...

52 The principle of intra-segment homogeneity vs. inter-segment heterogeneity

53 'The Marketing Dictionary', Fifth edition 1996, Norman Hart, Butterworth Heinemann CIM series.

54 Compared to the average size for that market

55 Morgan cars, for example

56 The author is not impugning the National Health Service, too few resources and too high a workload means that people in the NHS on all sides are under a pressure that militates against providing the same levels of care and attention to patients as can be provided by the private sector. The author has cause to know this well, having the experience of receiving trauma care in a range of hospitals during his lifetime, both in the Navy, NHS and private sectors.

57 'The Times', Business Travel, April 27, 1995

58 i.e. how personality translates into behaviour. There are said to be some 650 plus personality traits, and because of this most marketers cluster these under crude headings, which are frequently labelled with some acronym from the descriptors, e.g. YUPPY – Young Upwardly Mobile Urban Professional, or DINK/Y = Dual Income, No Kids/Yet, WOOPies – Well Off Older People etc, OR the four Cs (Categories?) of Young and Rubicam's classification, 'Mainstream', 'Achievers', 'Succeeders', and 'Reformers', each of whom have different psychological drives that dominate their buying behaviour.

59 The components of which are usually considered to be the person's work and leisure activities, interests and opinions

60 The technique is also being extended to urban areas of Western Europe and North America

ELEVEN

Promoting a service

ELEVEN

Promoting a service

Introduction

"If you have a competitive advantage, shout it from the roof tops, if not, then shut up until you do."

After Malcolm MacDonald

"If the idea is present, there is not much work for the brush to do."

Japanese calligraphic dictum

It's not the purpose of this chapter to replace or summarize the plethora of other work that has been published, some in this series, on the many and varied disciplines associated with marketing promotion. These range from advertising to exhibitions, writing copy, to media buying, they are all relevant here. And they apply equally as much to goods as to services. The purpose of this chapter is to focus on two specific areas of promoting a service business: 'Tactical' and 'Close Quarter', each of which are critical to the service sector today.

The tactical issue highlighted is 'editorial publicity' an aspect of public relations.

The close quarter techniques will outline the necessary activities for networking/connections.

Editorial publicity

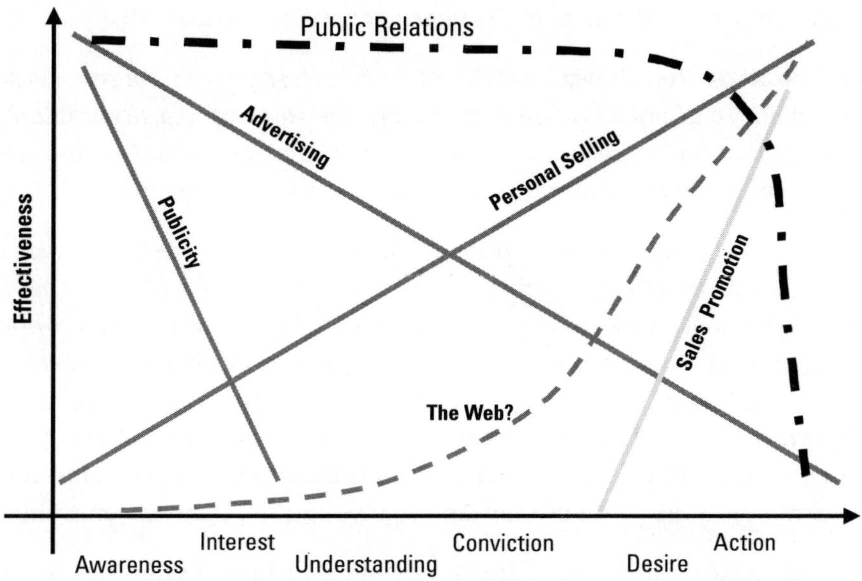

FIG 11.1: THE PROMOTIONS MIX

Fig 11.1 is sometimes referred to as the 'DAGMAR Model', which stands for Define Advertising Goals for Measured Advertising Results. The model purports to show the role of each element of the promotions mix in moving the customer towards the sale. The vertical axis shows an arbitrary measure of effectiveness and the horizontal axis shows the process, moving from the prospect becoming aware of the firm, to making the sale.

Off the figure and to the left, the potential customer is only a 'suspect' because he or she is unaware. So the first role of any promotions campaign is to create awareness. This can be measured, which makes 'awareness' a very useful criteria, or goal, by which to assess a campaign (at least in the early stages).

Moving to the right, the customer's awareness is heightened by creating 'understanding' or 'comprehension'. It's only when potential customers understand what the promotion is talking about that they can be interested in it. The next job in any promotional campaign is to convert that interest into a conviction that the promoted service is right for the customer. However, potential customers (at this stage of the process referred to as 'prospects') are rarely in the market for what is being promoted when they first hear about it. So having raised awareness, created understanding, interest and desire, it is critical that these are maintained (i.e. the prospect is not allowed to forget) until they are looking to buy. At that point they are in the market for the service and it's then up to the promotions mix to close that sale.

Working across from the left hand side of Fig 11.1 it can be seen that advertising and publicity (such things as exhibitions and sponsorship) are extraordinarily good at creating awareness but that their effectiveness in making the sale tails off dramatically as the customer progresses towards the right.

However, still at the left hand edge of Figure 11.1 we also see that personal selling is most ineffective when it comes to creating awareness. This is frequently manifest via an activity known as cold calling, where sales people are employed to generate leads. Because of the inevitable number of rejections encountered, nothing can be more disheartening from a sales point of view. This level of rejection does not affect sales people who have thick enough skins, but for the large majority this activity can be guaranteed to lower morale more certainly than almost anything else they may encounter.

Further, on the right side of Figure 11.1, the situation between personal selling and advertising is reversed. Nothing is more effective at closing a sale than a person-to-person encounter. That's not to say that services cannot be sold 'off the page', they can, and quite frequently are. But the page cannot answer questions, the page cannot build up rapport, the page cannot be seen as being reliable.

The main issue arising from the above figure is the relationship of the straight line elements in the promotion mix with the curved line element, which we've labelled 'Public Relations/Editorial Publicity'. Public Relations (PR) in its wider context is a highly strategic element of the total promotions mix. However, this chapter wishes to focus on the more tactical element, 'editorial publicity', which is a subset of the larger PR picture.

Editorial publicity is where editorial is published about one's service product. This editorial appears in media (print or broadcast) that are 'consumed[61]' by the marketer's target audience.

What makes editorial publicity so attractive to the service marketer is its cost effectiveness.

There are two issues here.

1. The first is the issue of cost itself.
2. The second is the issue of effectiveness or credibility in this context.

With regards to cost, Editorial Publicity *is not free*, but it is many orders of magnitude less expensive than any other element of the promotions mix, and the effectiveness of this expenditure is enhanced enormously by the very high levels of credibility that can be obtained[62].

Editorial Publicity can create and build awareness more cost effectively than almost anything known. Experience shows that most readers will more readily scan the editorial headlines and read the text that follows than they will the advertisements or advertorials. Audiences have an annoying tendency to skip the ads, both in the printed and the broadcast media (unless they are specifically interested in a particular topic, or perhaps in the market for that service).

There is nothing more effective than editorial publicity in building understanding, interest and conviction, as can be seen from Figure 11.1 above because editorial publicity carries far more credibility than any advertorial or advertising can buy. The reason for this is that the audience perceives the editorial as being produced by an objective observer, someone like themselves. Advertorials or adverts are received with a healthy seasoning of what Mandy Rice-Davies once referred to as "Well they would say that, wouldn't they?".

Editorial publicity can therefore put over a point of view in the most effective manner.

As also can be seen from Figure 11.1, the effectiveness of editorial publicity tails off dramatically from conviction through to action. This author is at a loss to understand why this should be the case, particularly since at the end of the copy there will be some form of contact address and telephone number. Could it be that because the generating organization view editorial publicity/public relations as 'strategic' (vs. 'tactical') they do not provide the resources and mechanisms, whereby any enquiries can be followed up? The author has specific experience that appears to confirm this conclusion, when following up editorial about a skiing holiday in 1997. A particularly laudatory article appeared in the skiing press about a Canadian resort. It concluded with contact telephone numbers, e-mail and internet addresses. But try as he may, the author could get no response whatsoever (was the resort only geared up to respond to the 'trade'?)

Similar situations have occurred when following up articles about where to eat: restaurants that have been cited as particularly good, not having the resources to answer the telephone or the phone being continually engaged. The list goes on.

Generating editorial publicity

Most service organizations that think about the use of editorial publicity usually only conceive of it as a reactive tool. In other words, when something happens that they believe is a newsworthy event, then and only then, will they take action to try and generate press interest in the topic. This we might refer to as taking advantage of 'targets of opportunity'.

However, the service organizations that are more successful in their use of editorial publicity tend to be **proactive**, they take charge of events, they generate their own news.

There's nothing mutually exclusive about these two approaches; in fact the author has found that the service organizations, which are the most successful at promoting themselves, have frequently combined the two. In other words, whilst setting out to generate their own news, they have kept an eye open for stories which they will exploit when they occur even though unanticipated.

Let's examine each of these in turn.

Targets of opportunity

Like most activities in life, success will depend on how much preparation has been put in beforehand. Einstein said, "Chance favours the prepared mind"; Gary Player said, "The harder I practice the luckier I get". And so it is with editorial publicity. The necessary preparation for EP is firstly knowing how to write a press release, (we deal with this later) and secondly, knowing to whom to send the press release and we will deal with that now.

Press releases can be sent off like pellets from a shotgun, everyone will get at least one. This can be an awful lot of work, create a tremendous amount of annoyance in the industry and be relatively ineffective, other than at close quarters.

Or a press release can target specific journals known for being leaders amongst their peers.

The successful service marketer will therefore study the style of these journalists study the topics that are of interest to them and establish contact by telephone. The call is designed to discover what best turns them on, how best to present the story to them, and what particular things about a press release will annoy them more than anything else. In other words, like all marketing, *know your customer*.

It's useful at this point to build a database of such journalists, cross referenced by areas of interest, media and the particular likes and dislikes of the people concerned. Then when the targets of opportunity arise, a series of pertinent and specifically tailored press releases can be dispatched in relatively short order.

However, the problem with the 'target of opportunity' approach quite simply is that by definition, the service marketer has no control over when the newsworthy event will occur. And from a journalist's point of view, it's very much like waiting for a London bus. A long time can go by waiting at the bus stop, then all of a sudden along come four together. So it is with newsworthy items.

Experience shows that frequently our own unanticipated news event will occur at, or around the same time, as similarly wonderful pieces of news from other organizations. It is said, that on a good day, journalists can receive as many as 80 to a 100 different press releases (a bad day is when no press releases are received). We need to adopt tactics to increase the probability that our press release will be used rather than the others (we address this later).

Proactive – EP strategies

The preparation under this strategy will include getting to know the journalists as before, but critical to this approach is also discovering when your industry's 'dog days' for news will occur. All industries have them; these are times of the year when nothing newsworthy appears to be happening. In some industries, this is known as the 'silly season', during which trivial issues are blown out of all proportion in order to generate stories that fill the page. However, knowing when these dog days occur, we can generate stories to break on or around these times and thus increase the chance of our news being covered.

Proactive news generation can entail two distinct approaches, which again are not mutually exclusive, the successful organization will combine the two:

- The first is the use of short-term events such as marketing research – and
- the second is to create publicity events specifically to generate news for the organization.

Marketing research

Every time an organization conducts any marketing, (or market) research,[63] it has a wonderful opportunity to generate newsworthy material. Indeed, this can be so effective in terms of the column inches or other coverage that is obtained, that the business could not have purchased that media space if it had used the research budget solely on buying advertising.

Hardly a day goes by where such activity cannot be seen to have taken place. Journals, newspapers and the broadcast media frequently carry stories, the first paragraph of which will start with words to the effect, "According to a recent survey carried out on behalf of... (*put your name in here*)". It will then go on to reveal such startling insights as, "olive oil prevents strokes", "Skiing is becoming a family sport", "More old people are private pilots today than at any time in history", etc.

Interestingly, the issues do not necessarily have to be directly connected with one's service or one's service products. But the news event must cite your particular organization and do so as frequently as possible.

The generation of such news requires the use of what are known as 'hook questions', included within whatever the research instrument[64] happens to be. These hook questions are generated in collaboration with the interested journalist and are designed specifically to produce news which will 'hook' their readers' attention.

Obtaining good hook questions is all part of the process of anticipation and preparation.

During the preparation stage, journalists are identified and contact with them is initiated. The successful service marketer who has in mind the possibility of using market research, will be especially on the look out for journalists who are opinion makers in their field. These journalists will be sounded out as to how receptive they might be to such an approach and, if receptive, some *modus vivendi* will be agreed, whereby both can work together on such news generation in the future.

The service marketer will try to be proactive with the market research diary so as to schedule products that can be used to generate news that will coincide with their service sector's industry dog days. Then, at least a month before the research instrument is designed, a limited number of the journalists that could be cooperative are approached with the following proposition:

In return for the exclusive rights to use the results produced by the two hook questions which they are to generate, and guaranteed source attribution[65], they will be provided with the hook question data, exclusively, and absolutely free of any cost. Most journalists would jump at the chance, the offer of an exclusive is almost universally irresistible.

It is absolutely vital to use at least two hook questions (it usually can't be more without detracting from the main purpose of the survey). The reason is that one question can sometimes fail to generate a sufficiently interesting response, or it may even generate a response, which will be impossible to publish.[66]

Newsworthy data gathering is not confined to market research. A critical part of marketing a service business is to establish a feedback loop whereby the business can stay in touch with the customers' level of satisfaction, expectations and trends – as well as other changes to the customer base over time. This we refer to as a 'Customer Information System', frequently abbreviated to CIS. When designing such a system, it is always wise to include data capture for issues that generate news stories, as well as monitor customer satisfaction and composition. So, if one ran a ski resort for example, the CIS would be capable of showing how:

- More and more families are skiing today than did three years ago,
- More and more British are skiing in America than are skiing in Europe, and
- That the main decision-maker as to which resort the family visits is now the woman in the family rather than the man, as traditionally used to be the case.

Which, the article would go on to postulate, had tremendous implications for the design of the modern ski resort. Not only in terms of its facilities at the base, but also in terms of the character of the ski runs. The emphasis should move away from testosterone generating moguls to wide sweeping pistes with phenomenal mountain views, trails going down between avenues of scented pine trees with slopes that are not too dangerous for the youngest members of the family to enjoy without fear of injury.[67]

Publicity events

A longer-term strategy of being proactive would be the organization of publicity events designed to generate on-going stories over, perhaps, a considerable period of time. One illustration of this technique will have to suffice.

Back in the late 1980s the author consulted for The Hospital Corporation of America (HCA). During which time he witnessed the design and use of their annual calendar to create a great deal of favourable publicity – that lasted over the span of three years.

The HCA calendar

HCA was a hospital group purchased in the early '90s from its American owners by the BUPA group. In the mid '80s it had some 12 to 14 hospitals spread throughout the United Kingdom. In 1985 and 1986 under the leadership of one of its more inspired hospital directors, (who later went on to become a marketing manager for a rival group), a one year campaign was designed and subsequently extended for two more years.

In brief, it consisted of running a painting competition in infant schools that were located within the catchment areas of each of the various HCA hospitals throughout the United Kingdom.

The theme of the competition was preventative health care and there were prizes for the top child in every school and the top child in the hospital's area. There was also a fairly large prize for the school attended by the winning child in each area.

Infant schools were chosen because there was a high probability that within this target audience, (i.e. well-off middle class with private medical health care insurance) mum would take the child to school. Therefore, each hospital could reach the families who mattered via the schools.

There was a considerable amount of media activity at two major occasions.

- Firstly at the launch, which included interviews with the press and broadcast media; then again at the end of the competition when prizes were awarded.
- By the second occasion, the competition had become a noteworthy local event and many more members of the media attended the resultant photo opportunities.

Winning paintings from each of the areas of the main 12 hospitals in the United Kingdom were featured as a picture, each to its own month in the 1987 calendar.

This calendar was distributed to 'influencers' in each of the hospital's catchment areas. These influencers comprised such professions and occupations as bank managers, doctors, vets, accountants, lawyers, barristers and estate agents.

The mail-out of the 1987 calendar occurred just before Christmas 1986. Each calendar was accompanied by a short note which expressed regret that it could not be delivered in person, however, someone from the hospital would be calling early in the New Year and if the calendar was found on the desk of the person to whom the letter was addressed, then they would receive half a bottle of champagne with the compliments of the hospital.

This mail-out was followed-up with a mystery shopping exercise by the research company and over 80 percent of all recipients of the mail-out that were visited, had this calendar on the desk eagerly awaiting their half bottle of champagne. (It's not recorded how many half bottles of champagne were actually distributed over that period of time.) Finally some bright spark in 1987 realized that the HCA had a valuable resource with which to continue the story into 1988 and 1989. This was done by selecting, from all the paintings that came second in each catchment area, enough pictures to form either a montage or a single card front. These were used by the hospital group to form the fronts of Christmas cards for 1988 and 1989.

The author has reason to believe that when these HCA hospitals were eventually sold a few years after the above promotion, the price paid to HCA for these UK hospitals included a considerable premium for 'goodwill', i.e. the customer franchise they had built-up over the years via the use of such innovative promotions.

BEWARE THAT YOU ARE ADDRESSING THE RIGHT AUDIENCE

The main issue in generating any publicity via an 'event' such as above, is that the event chosen must be of interest to the target group of customers to whom the service is marketed.

An illustration of getting this dramatically wrong was in the mid '80s when Royal Mail Datapost sponsored Formula Three sports car racing for several years.

Although this generated a lot of PR in the racing press it didn't increase awareness, understanding or interest amongst its main target groups, i.e. those people in organizations that are responsible for the mailroom.

These people, it appeared, had absolutely no interest in Formula Three sports car racing and in fact, subsequent research discovered that many of the target group didn't even know that such a sport category existed.

Communication channels for editorial publicity

There are three main categories for communicating editorial publicity for a service business to its target group. They are:

- printed editorial, such as newspapers and journals,
- broadcast editorial, such as television or radio, and
- internally generated channels mainly in the form of newsletters.

External media

This consists of print and broadcast media, both local and national.

Here the aim should be:

- Firstly to get editorial publicity of the type that would be stimulated by the press releases to be discussed, and

- Secondly, to make one or two people in the business (at the most), known to the press as good potential members of panels.

This is particularly relevant to broadcast media. An example of this would be a member of the firm who, over time, becomes well known to the public. They would appear on panels such as the judgment panel for selecting the local business person of the year, or participate in local game shows, and maybe even join bodies of local worthies that are consulted on-air over issues of local importance.

There is also 'rent-a-comment'; This is a strategy whereby an 'expert' in your organization is known as not only being informed on topics that may be of interest to the press, but also for the attractive and perhaps even controversial way in which they are capable of expressing a view. Thus when a particular event occurs that could well be supplemented by an informed, may be even 'expert' opinion, the journalist will contact this person, explain the context and ask for some view to be expressed.

Newsletters

These can form a very effective channel of communication with your marketplace if done with care.

This channel falls into four main categories:

1. Marketers comment
2. In-house newsletters
3. Lifestyle newsletters, and
4. Audio magazines.

Of the three categories, 'in-house newsletters' are the most ineffective, primarily because they consist of puffs glorifying the wonders of an organization. They feature photographs of luminaries inside the firm, talking about wonderful new contracts that the firm has won and perhaps occasionally, they include small case histories of how satisfied their clients are with the firm. **The world is full of this type of glossy.**

If there is any use left for this category it is for internal communications within an organization. Here people can see themselves praised, show photographs of themselves to their loved ones and colleagues, and management can communicate to their employees in a more glitzy way about the issues that face the firm.

A lifestyle magazine, however, is where a large portion of the published document is devoted to issues other than those glorifying the firm. These topics are selected on their attractiveness to the target group in question so that the intended audience will read the magazine, perhaps even circulate it amongst their friends and some might even collect it.

Once the lifestyle magazine's design is working it can afford to feature a few advertorials here and there, and even the occasional advertisement.

A good example of this was the Toplist Magazine used by CFH[68] to add value to its computer listing paper. The paper was boxed and the magazine enclosed therein. Toplist brand managers had discovered that the main decision-maker as to whose computer listing paper to buy was the person in charge of loading the printers before the usual long overnight print run, and there was only a slight price differential between the competing brands[69]. This proved a useful conduit for promotion. It helped to launch several new products including pre-printed stationery and other items in the CFH range.

Audio magazines in the form of compact tape cassettes have the previous two types of newsletters beaten hollow. At the time of writing the use of audio cassettes in the United Kingdom is still very much in its infancy, but one only has to look at the alacrity with which they are accepted in the United States of America to appreciate the tremendous potential that exists.

The main benefit they offer the publisher is that the audience can consume the tape whilst doing something else. In other words, the tape enables the listener to use their time twice. They can listen to the tape whilst walking, driving the car (perhaps the most popular), gardening, in the bath, decorating and any other form of DIY.

As far as the author is concerned there is only one area he's discovered so far that precludes the use of the tape at the same time and that is swimming, particularly the underwater variety.

The author is aware of several organizations successfully using audio tapes as internal newsletters, notable amongst which was the Norwich Union group who used tapes to communicate effectively with their Independent Financial Advisors (IFAs), brokers and sales force. There are even producers, such as the former 'Business Sound' of Guildford, England, who specialize in producing tapes for companies both for internal communications and also for communicating with other relevant audiences.

Business Sound produced a monthly tape magazine, known as *Executive Briefing*, the content of which comprised articles across the range of business interest, from advice on pricing, briefings and updates on employment law, expert opinion with snippets on marketing, new production techniques and, occasionally, a humorous article or two.

The main issues to be addressed for the successful use of an audiotape magazine are the quality of the sound on the tape and the 'audio variety'[70] of the content.

One of the factors that has held back the progress of audio magazines in the United Kingdom, is the belief held by many people that these can be produced on a home cassette tape recorder. The sound quality of the subsequent publication is appalling and serves to deter rather than attract an audience.

The press release[71]

The success of much that has preceded in this chapter will hinge largely on the skill with which the organization has been able to issue a press release. This tool is not one that is too difficult to use.

The good press release depends on the service marketer adhering to some simple principles and employing the checklist, which follows in more detail below.

The press release checklist

- Date
- Preferably on headed paper
- Head it **'press release'**
- Outstanding quality of size and paper
- Use of colour within the text to highlight and make visually appealing (with care)
- Give address, phone no., name of contact

Continued over...

The press release checklist *continued*

- Say when to be used (or embargoed etc.)
- Short simple relevant headline
- Answer 5 x W's + H
- Accompany it with good photographs
- Use 'verbatims' where possible
- Human touch (+ local angle if relevant)
- Don't carry paras. onto next page
- 'More' at end of pages, 'End' at end
- Leave plenty of space, margins, between lines and paragraphs etc.
- Concise and precise text – with simple language.

Re. journalists with older eyes

- Use large(ish) type face [i.e. >13pt]
- DO NOT include small numbers and brackets!
- Insert the words 'PRESS RELEASE' immediately after the heading
- Say when to be used (or embargoed etc.)
- Use OUTSTANDING quality and size of paper
- To build visual appeal – Use colour with text to highlight – but with care!
- KEEP IT TO ONE PAGE if possible
- TITLE; Times Roman or 'Schoolbook'
- **MAKE SURE IT GETS THERE**

Networking and making connections

"In the network environment rewards come by empowering others not climbing over them."

John Naisbitt in 'Mega Trends'

When marketing professional services or those services with a very high content level of intellectual property, skill at 'networking' is absolutely vital. There used to be an old saying, *"It's not what you know that is important, but who you know"*, although relevant, this is not the whole story, it's not even the most important part of the story. The marketer of professional services must always bear in mind that the objective is: **TO MANAGE WHO KNOWS THEM. This is an intrinsically difficult thing to do, because almost by definition, more people will know of your organization that it is possible for your organization to know.**

So the service marketer must employ a strategy designed to stay in touch with as many people as possible and try and create an environment whereby those with whom they are in contact will spread the good news outside the boundaries that delineate the extent of the service marketer's control.

Objectives

The intention of any networking activity is not to build a high social professional profile, as many believe, though this may well be a bi-product and, for some people, prove quite enjoyable.

The objectives are, however, to build and maintain:

- The organization's connection to the grapevine, (the network) via:
- Building databases specific to the service marketer's firm. The whole principle was beautifully stated many years ago by Mark H. McCormack in his rubric, "He who has the largest Roladex wins", of course, Roladex's are now old hat, the firm must employ a modern computer (PC) database, but the principle still applies.

The context of managing who knows you

A short definition is useful here: networking is the activity that builds connections on the grapevine for people or organizations. A connection is a known individual on the database. It is not a full and useful connection, however, until contact details are obtained and recorded in some easily referenced format. It is always useful to collect other information to flesh out what is known about the person, but it should never be forgotten that a database is a reference tool *not a dossier*.

In Figure 11.2, we see where networking fits in to the overall promotional activity of the service organization. At the top of the tree we have the sales plan, which in this context divides into two distinctly different activities.

- One is support activity, such as advertising, PR, editorial publicity, already mentioned.
- The other is sales activity which is designed to influence purchase via a person-to-person process.

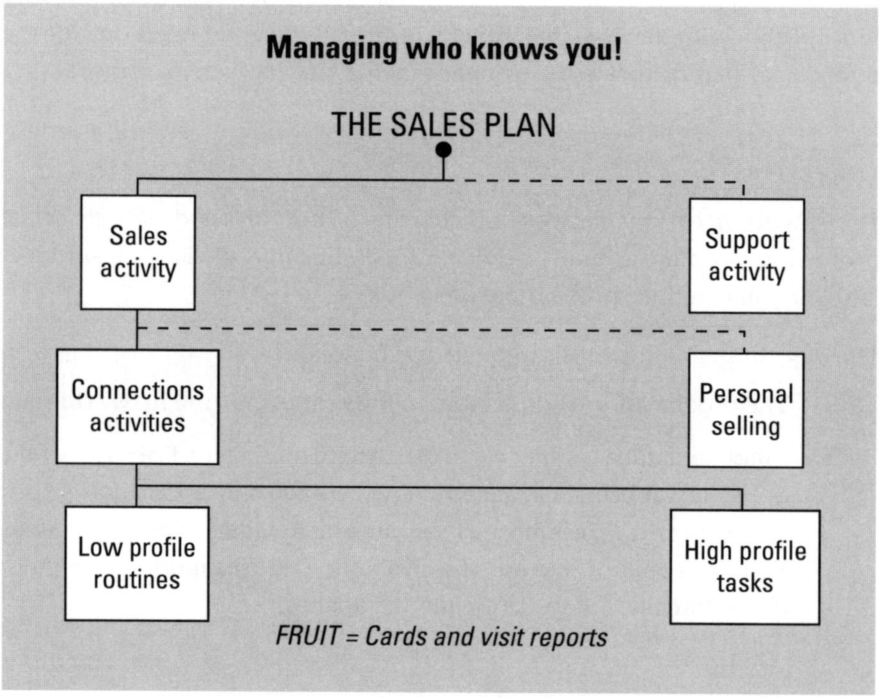

FIG 11.2: THE CONNECTIONS TREE

At the intellectual property end of the Service Spectrum (Chapter 2, Fig 2.2) these sales activities will have two distinctly different components. These are:

- personal selling, and
- connections.

Selling activities can be characterized by situations where both parties are fully aware of the purpose of the meeting.

That is to say that the purpose of one part is to communicate and persuade as effectively as possible, and the responsibility of the other is to buy, in a professional and a mature way, so as to maximize the value and minimize the cost of this purchase. Whilst selling is not an unfriendly activity, there is a certain ambience of 'confrontation' that will be created under these circumstances which is alien to making connections.

The purpose of connection (or networking) activities is to either:

- create opportunities via making a connection to a person who might be able to purchase or influence a purchase at some time in the future, or
- to make a connection to someone who can, in turn, connect you with someone else who can buy at sometime in the future.

In addition to buying opportunities, handled properly, the grapevine is a phenomenally useful source of information. Thus a major purpose of networking, particularly in professional services, is to ensure that the business is kept in the picture about what is happening in the marketplace.

Networking activities themselves break down into two clear categories.

- Firstly, there are the low profile routines, which are analogous to what the police term routine legwork or what Bernard Shaw referred to as "99% perspiration". These routines provide the solid bedrock foundation, which is so necessary if the second category of networking activity, high profile tasks, is to flourish.
- Secondly, the 'high profile tasks' – the objectives of which are to create, for the business, the 'brand', reputation, public values (i.e. what the firm stands for).

Low profile routines

This category of networking activity consists of a schedule of regular disciplined and systematic activity designed to maximize the interface between the organization and its professional environment.

The service marketer makes it work by getting the relevant people in the organization, (those with the right aptitudes who are at the right organizational level and who have the pertinent technical skills and/or professional qualifications, (if relevant)) to take responsibility for maintaining contact and relationship activities with specific professional bodies.

For example, lets say that Tom Brown will be responsible for keeping contact with the Mechanical Engineering and the Concrete Engineer's Society, Fred Smith will be responsible for keeping contact with the Institute of Electrical Engineering and the Association of Software Writers; Fred Bloggs will make contact on behalf of the organization with such bodies as the Chartered Institute of Marketing and the Marketing Society. The list goes on...

The emphasis is not that they should personally turn up to all the meetings, but they should make sure that at every open meeting of the 'allocated' professional body somebody from the organization is *present*. At these meetings, the person attending will circulate, will socialise, will exchange 'scuttlebutt' (not so trivial as gossip), with those present and exchange cards with any new contacts, or with those people who tell them that their circumstances (addresses, telephone numbers, companies who employ them and so forth) have changed.

It is absolutely vital that people who participate in low profile routines are always equipped with copious amounts of business cards. The purpose is not to give out as many cards as possible, although that is always useful, the main objective is to gather other people's cards via exchanging them with yours.

How our cards are used is outside our control once we have given them away in exchange for somebody else's card.

The fruit of low profile routines therefore is a series of concise visit reports which are put into the organizational system together with any newly obtained cards that need to be entered into the database.

The low profile routine activity has not been completed until the people involved have fed into the system any visit reports (circa 300 words max.), so that later on it can be searched and collated according to key word search criteria.

Secondly, perhaps even more important, the suitably classified cards can be fed into the system, thus building the database. The sort of classifications that might be given to cards are such that at the top end of the spectrum they would warrant an immediate response to the prior event with some form of letter saying 'nice to have met you' (etc). Perhaps even including some sales literature to bring the contact up to date. Slightly lower down on the spectrum would be an instruction to arrange a formal appointment at some time in the future.

Moving down in terms of priorities, put the cards' data on the mailing list, classified as to the topics under which they will be headed, whether they are for just general or specific types of mailing, (including such things as greetings cards) or, if the contact is particular intimate, let's say birthday cards.

And finally the connection is classified as to the frequency with which the contact ought to be refreshed.

High profile tasks

So much for the mundane low profile activities, these are very important, they provide the foundation, but the high profile tasks provide the glory.

The purpose of high profile tasks is to increase the visibility of an organization, to raise its profile with its target group, via employing activities which in one way or another all amount to the same thing, publishing.

When detailing people to participate in the high profile tasks it is important to ensure that they have suitable aptitudes. These sort of tasks require people who have no fear of public speaking, who are in effect extroverts. In some circumstances the firm will also require people who can author and/or can present particularly well.

At its most mundane, these activities will involve such people being members of a committee on the 'professional body'. The aim being to eventually take some office of responsibility on a committee, or two, perhaps even a 'Chair'. This will ensure high profile participation at a multitude of events connected both with the internal management of the professional body and its external activities.

Moving up the scale of importance, high profile tasks would include things like presenting papers at seminars, publishing books, writing articles with the specific intention of raising the personal profile of the author and, through association, the profile of the service firm concerned.

Finally, there is the presentation of papers, carrying out training and becoming known as an authority within the industry as a 'rent-a-quote'. Perhaps also a visiting professorship, one can never aim too high.

Exercise

1. With your management team make a list of all the professional or trade bodies that impinge on the activities of your service business:
   - directly in terms of the professional skills you require in-house, or
   - indirectly, in terms of the sorts of professions practiced by your target customers (e.g. your credibility as a supplier to the hospitality industry can be enhanced by being a member of, say, 'The Licensed Victuallers Association'; or for an accountancy practice, 'The Institute of Chartered Accountants').
2. At how many of these is your business:
   - adequately represented on the committee – at least at local level?
   - represented by someone from the business regularly attending, say > 50% of all meetings/branch meetings?
   - represented at any of the annual conferences?
3. Priority must be given to addressing any of the above issues where the response indicated that a real gap existed in your professional and/or trade profile.

   ASSUMING THE ABOVE IS NOT ALL NEGATIVE:
   - How many live contacts/connections do you have with other members of these industry bodies at:
     - local level?
     - national level?
4. In light of the second half of this chapter, what are your strategies and plans to exploit or ameliorate the situation you have discovered above?

References

61 *Read, understood, believed and acted upon.*

62 *Perhaps one of the best practical guides to the generation of editorial publicity is Michael Bland's book, "Be Your Own PR Man", Kogan Page Ltd., paperback edition 1983 onwards.*

63 *See Chapter 13 for a definition of the difference between Market vs Marketing Research*

64 *i.e. Questionnaires, diaries, focus group discussions et al.*

65 *i.e. the Service Marketer's organization is cited within the story, several times if possible*

66 *The author has several examples from his own experience over the years, though there is not space here to elaborate. The foreword to this book features the author's website and his email address, he would be delighted to provide these examples if requested.*

67 *This is an actual news story that appeared in the newspaper USA Today in the late 90s*

68 *Continue Forms Holdings Ltd*

69 *Details of this story omitted due to lack of space, but available on request.*

70 *For 'Audio Variety' read easy to listen to, makes it entertaining. Short articles, interviews, a range of differing voices, some music at intro, outro and occasionally between.*

71 *For more details re. methodology see 'Be Your Own PR Man' Michael Bland, Kogan Page, 1986*

TWELVE

Pricing a service

TWELVE
Pricing a service

Introduction

"How high does profit have to be before we call it immoral – if it's so low that we have to lay people off, how moral can that be?"

John Wrinkler

This chapter surveys some of the more service specific issues that a marketer must take into account when deciding on the pricing strategy for their service business. It continues by examining some potential conventional market pricing strategies, all are revised, as are the implications that the ratios of overhead to variable cost will have on the strategies to be adopted.[72]

Executive multiplier considerations

The concept of the executive multiplier is important particularly for those services where intellectual property is a critical element of the offering. This intellectual property usually resides in the hands of one or two people central to the organization. The success of the business depends on how effectively this know-how can be multiplied via the employment of individuals who may not be as skilled as the principals but who can work under the guidance of those who are.

The concept for example, is that one good chef via training and supervision can employ staff to multiply the effectiveness of his/her skills and run a considerable restaurant. Whereas if that chef were to work just on his/her own, there would be a limit as to the amount of work that could be done and therefore the money that that one chef could earn. Similarly with a market research firm: one or two skilled market research executives employing a suitable administrative staff can multiply the effect of their skills out of all proportion to the amount of work that they would otherwise be able to do if they were on their own.

As can be seen in Figure 12.1, the ability to use the executive multiplier concept depends very much on whereabouts in the Service Spectrum the service business is located.

As can be seen, towards the left hand edge of the spectrum, good chefs, good market researchers, good consultants, good accountants, can act in a way very similar to that of an officer in an armed force who uses their troops to multiply the effect of their insights and their strategies for the achievement of the objective.

An overlay on this situation is the use of differential pricing. The customer would have one price to deal with the 'indians', albeit under the control and responsibility of the 'chief' (i.e. the entrepreneur), but if that customer wanted to deal with the entrepreneur directly, then they would probably have to pay more.

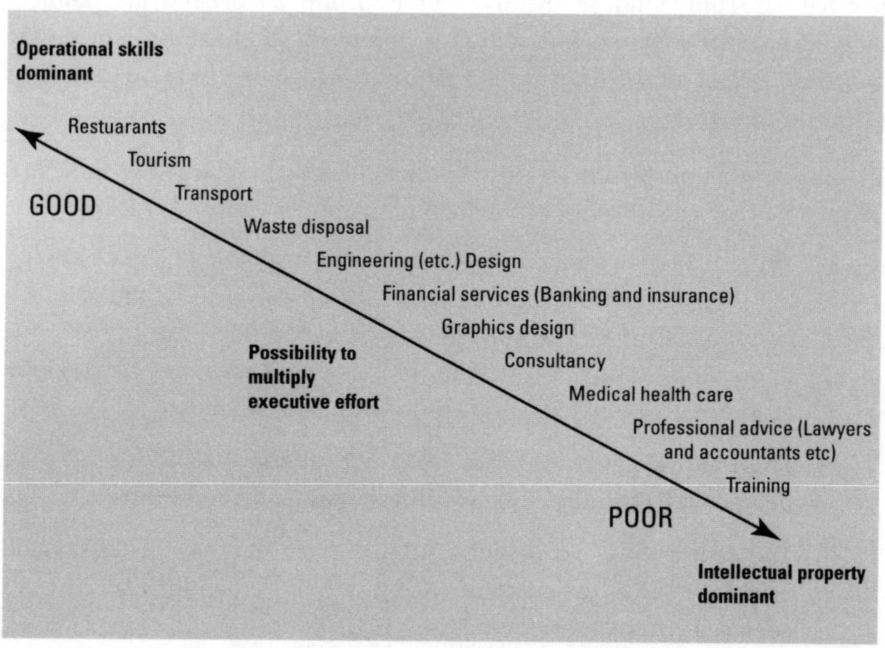

FIG 12.1: THE SERVICES SPECTRUM AND EXECUTIVE MULTIPLIER

However, the further one moves towards the intellectual property end of the spectrum, (i.e. the right hand side), then the less it becomes possible to use this concept in running the business. Thus for professional advice businesses, such as solicitors or barristers, or perhaps trainers, their customers require direct contact with the entrepreneur and no substitutes are accepted. A barrister can only be in one court at a time; a trainer may only be in front of one group of people at a time.

Some slight multiplication is of course always possible, in that barristers can write opinions out of hours and trainers, as in this example, can write books about their topic. Both of which activities have the advantage of earning money whilst the trainer or the barrister are on other stages at the time.

Price as an indicator of service quality

It is received wisdom in marketing that, under the right condition, price can often be a major indicator to customers or consumers of the quality of the products for sale. Nowhere is this more true than in the service sector.

Service is not only intangible and therefore prone to a great deal of subjectivity in its appraisal, but in addition it cannot be sampled. So, before the purchase, much of the offering is a promise which can only be evaluated after commitment.

The basic conditions that must exist for customers to use price as an indicator of quality are if one or more of the following apply:

- There is little or no product information available to the customer. In other words the customer is essentially naïve about the product, is unable to make an informed judgment and if the purchase is important enough, it's enough to make sure that they get it right, therefore, they will use price to inform their behaviour.
- There either may be no other evaluative criteria available or there are perceived to be major quality differences between brands.
- The issue is the word 'perceived'. The service marketer's battleground is in the mind of the customer and it is their perceptions, as we have seen elsewhere, that govern their behaviour.

- If the cost consequences of making bad decisions are great, and/or if the product has a high level of socio-economic significance. In both these situations the customer is apt to perceive a high level of risk.
- The buyers and/or other important members of the decision-making unit have confidence that price in their marketplace is an indicator of quality.

Services that are located towards the intellectual property end of the Service Spectrum are considered to be high in the need for credibility. In these services, price remains an important factor as an indicator of quality after consumption.

The greater the perceived risk and cost of a service going wrong, particularly if that affects the customers' view of their own particular worth, (that is to say it is socially visible) the greater the chance that a price reduction can demand the image of the service product. The service marketer should give a great deal of thought to any contemplated price reductions. They could detrimentally affect the image of the service product via hurting the egos of those who have already purchased.

If a service is of relatively short duration (i.e. it doesn't take a long time to deliver), but it yields benefits over a much longer period, for example, in terms of training or consultancy, the service marketer must include strategies to drive home the long-term investment nature of the service product, as a means of supporting the price.

Basic pricing strategies

Before identifying which are of particular use to the service marketer. It would be useful at this stage just to revisit the classic pricing strategies together with brief explanations as to their workings and benefits.

PENETRATION PRICING

This price helps the marketer get into a new marketplace.

PREMIUM PRICING

A high price designed to reinforce strategies that put the product at the top of its marketplace – specifically used in markets where price is seen as an indicator of quality, such as perfumes.

PRICE SKIMMING

This strategy starts off as premium price, but is deliberately designed to come down over time to anticipate or react to competitive or other pressures in the market. As its name implies, it takes the cream from the top of the market, it can also be used as a means of 'shepherding' demand and thereby relieving the pressures on resource capacity.

PROMOTIONAL PRICING

Designed to support all other marketing activity that may be involved in a particular promotion, such as, advertising, PR, special deals at distributors and so forth.

LINE PRICING

This is designed to reflect the position of a service product in the range of products on offer from that supplier so that at the top of the range the prices would be premium, at the bottom of the range they would be the lowest possible, and products between these two extremes would be priced pro rata.

The following strategies have particular relevance to pricing in the service sector.

BAIT PRICING

A pricing strategy that is designed to make it relatively cheap for a customer to enter the market by offering a low price for the very basic and standard version of the service product. The customer is then free or indeed, may be encouraged to add extras, at an increased price of course, from a menu of added options. A good example of this would be a chain of hotels designed specifically for the business community. The quoted price for a room would give the occupant a basic level of accommodation, but no more. If they wished to watch the television, that's extra, if they wished to have breakfast in the hotel, again that's extra.

DUAL OR MULTIPLE PRICING

This is where it is essentially the same service product, particularly with respect to the 'core' and the 'expected' parts, and maybe even for a substantial proportion of the 'augmented'. These products, however, are marketed to different segments and each segment has its own price which will be different from any other segment, some higher, some lower.

This strategy can only be successful if it is difficult, if not impossible, for one set of customers in one segment to communicate and/or compare their product offering with other customers in a different segment. This can be brought about by ensuring that one set of customers cannot even meet up with any other segments, or alternatively, even if they do, it is very difficult to compare one offering in their segment with the offerings in others. A good example of this is the segmentation policy that airlines employ. All passengers are accommodated within the same aluminum tube when flying from one airport to another; they all take off and land at the same time, hopefully.

However, the airline marketer has made it possible to charge substantially more for those people who sit in front of the aircraft compared to those people who sit in the back. They can do this because Business Class and First Class are usually provided with substantial augmentation to the product, i.e. wider seats, free drinks, more space, more luxurious toilets, passengers are allowed to get on and off the aircraft first and may often have different menus provided for their entertainment and their refreshments. All with a lower probability of being 'bounced' (i.e. moved to a later flight).

(We will revisit this situation later when talking about the ratio between overhead and variable costs in a service business.)

Finally, a service marketer can use dual pricing when they develop a 'fighter brand'. This policy is to launch a product specifically to do damage to a competitor via the use of low, sometimes even predatory prices. When the objective is accomplished and the competitor either withdraws or is reduced to bankruptcy, a service marketer will kill off the fighter brand and resume business with the main product, without having damaged its image as a consequence of the battle.

BARRIER PRICING

As we have seen when we examined the effect of product life cycle on pricing strategy, this is a pricing policy that is designed to make the marketplace unattractive for competitors to enter by being very unprofitable.

PREDATORY PRICING

This is a policy designed by the service marketer to put competitors out of a marketplace. In some countries this is illegal, but not (on the whole) in the United Kingdom.

A good example of the employment of 'predatory pricing' was the battle that occurred in 1996 between *The Times* and *The Daily Telegraph* (on the one side) and the Independent (on the other). During a major part of that year, *The Times* and the *Telegraph* aimed aggressive predatory pricing strategies against

The Independent in the hopes of driving it out of the market. However, after some dramatic re-organization, the Board of *The Independent* was able to link up with a syndicate of other European newspapers for support and thus increased the size of its war chest and the depth of its pockets.

A consequence was that, faced with the prospect of a long and costly war of attrition, *The Times* and *The Telegraph*, ceased their pricing policy. It is interesting to note that this episode served to increase the overall circulation of broadsheet newspapers in the United Kingdom, whilst at the same time, proving a salutary experience to *The Independent* who, by the end of 1997, had repositioned itself out of the segment that put it in direct competition with *The Times* and *The Telegraph*, and into the segment occupied by *The Guardian*, the only national broadsheet (apart from *The Financial Times*) that had not been adversely affected by the former predatory pricing war.

Specific strategies for service pricing

Price as a shepherd

The service marketer may require to relieve pressure on resources, or to channel customers into one segment rather than other. For example, for travel services a premium price can be used at peak times and a highly discounted price for other times of the day. In those services where a great deal of social interaction takes place, varying the price of a service, can vary the types of people that use it. In those services which are characterized by having high levels of inter-customer contact and involvement, and/or where customers use other customers as an indicator of the quality of the service that they are contemplating, to mix the wrong sorts of people on any one occasion in any one service can have a very negative effect on the perception of its quality. So the service marketer will use price to attract one set of people to the up-market end of the product range, whilst deterring, via the use of price, those who would not be accepted in this segment. A good example of this being the segregation of those attending a horse race where the 'Silver Ring' enclosure is cheaper than the 'Member's enclosure, and a lot less 'select'.

Relationship/partnership pricing

The intention of this pricing strategy is to build long-term relationships. The strategy itself comprises several objectives, one being to raise the barriers to entry for competitors and the other, ironically, is to raise the hurdle of pain that would have to be overcome by customers who may be contemplating placing their business elsewhere.

The relationship/partnership pricing strategy consists of four main parts:

- **Firstly**, usually a 'Service Level Agreement' between the two (or more) parties. This would set out agreed delivery times, speeds of response, levels of availability, cleanliness of vehicles say, frequency of meetings, the level of tolerance for faults, missed deliveries and so forth.
- **Secondly**, it would include open book accounting between the parties involved, so that the service provider can charge all agreed and certifiable costs as incurred.
- **Thirdly**, there would usually be a management fee (frequently negotiated on an annual basis). This is sometimes negotiated as an agreed ratio of overall expenditure, as for example in several large and famous advertising agencies, or a fixed monetary amount as perhaps might be the case for a firm providing hauler services.
- **Finally**, there would be a performance bonus, this again would be negotiated, also perhaps on an annual or some other periodic basis. The bonus being tied directly to the supplier's performance against the service level agreement as above.

The principle behind the following structure is that with the costs and management fee, the service provider can only break-even. To make any profit at all they will have to perform up to and beyond the service leveled agreement, and receive the bonuses that have been negotiated.

The instance of relationship pricing is on the increase in the service industry particularly amongst those firms providing business-to-business services for which the customer would have a constant requirement. A particularly good example of a relationship pricing strategy is to be found in the BBC video of the Tom Peter's presentation *Management Imagination*. It cites the case of Lanes Transport of Bristol and their pricing arrangements with The Body Shop organization (this being the last case study of the four cited in that publication).

Cost structure considerations for pricing services

Cost plus

Cost plus systems of pricing in any business are perhaps the easiest things to do. They look the most logical and yet can lead to terrible problems, particularly in all but the simplest of company structures. The most important thing to appreciate is that it is inordinately difficult to decide what the actual cost is. For a multi service/product company, the so-called 'fixed costs' per product, transaction or relationship can be no more than an opinion based on that particular firm's 'attribution' policies. (Just as price is a policy based on an opinion of the effect it will have on the attainment of the firm's market/business objectives.)

If we consider Figure 12.2 below, it looks so reasonable at price one where we break-even. Were we to charge a slightly lower price, we would break-even later and if a slightly higher price were introduced, we would break-even earlier. But the problem is that the characteristics of service such as their intangibility, inseparability and heterogeneity all make it very difficult, perhaps in some cases even impossible to calculate the real costs of providing any one-service episode.

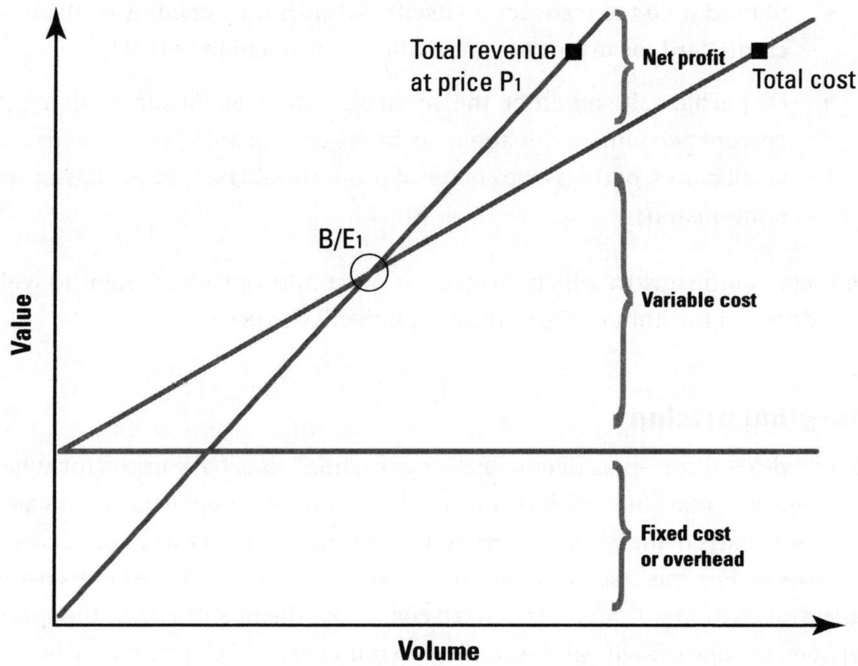

FIG 12.2: SIMPLE BREAK-EVEN

The service industry is rife with examples of catastrophic decisions being taken as a result of misleading overhead allocation. At one time, a major UK bank, nearly tore itself apart because of the way overheads, particularly those from branches, were allocated across the organization. The accountants at the top of the organization were ex-branch people and the regime that they had established was to allocate overhead according to the ratio of turnover of that part of the business, i.e. by branch. So the more turnover a particular part of the business did, the more of the overhead it actually carried. But corporate banking, whose main business was to provide cash transfer for client organizations, required no branch network, had an extremely high turnover and therefore carried a disproportionately unfair amount of the bank's overhead. Eventually the extent of this attribution made corporate banking uncompetitive in the marketplace.

Add to all the foregoing the question as to what is the actual profit center of a service business that has a wide range of products and activities.

- Should it be the branches, for examples, where the service is actually delivered?

- Should it be the transaction itself, like cashing a cheque, or using a credit card, or using the automatic teller machine (ATM)?
- Or perhaps, it should be the service product, like insurance, or the current account, or yet again, as in the case of some very successful small banks, perhaps the center of profit should be the total customer relationship.

All these options as to which strategy is most appropriate should be well considered in the light of the marketing objectives agreed.

Marginal pricing

Faced with the cost–plus dilemma, many organizations have opted for what is known as a 'marginal pricing' approach. Perhaps no more enthusiastically, as in some parts of the service industry such as market research or consultancy businesses. For this approach, as we can see in Figure 12.3, variable cost is placed on the bottom axis and the fixed cost or overhead is drawn as the space between the line drawn parallel to the variable cost line. 'Contribution' is that amount in excess of variable cost (i.e. the margin) that the organization is able to charge its customers.

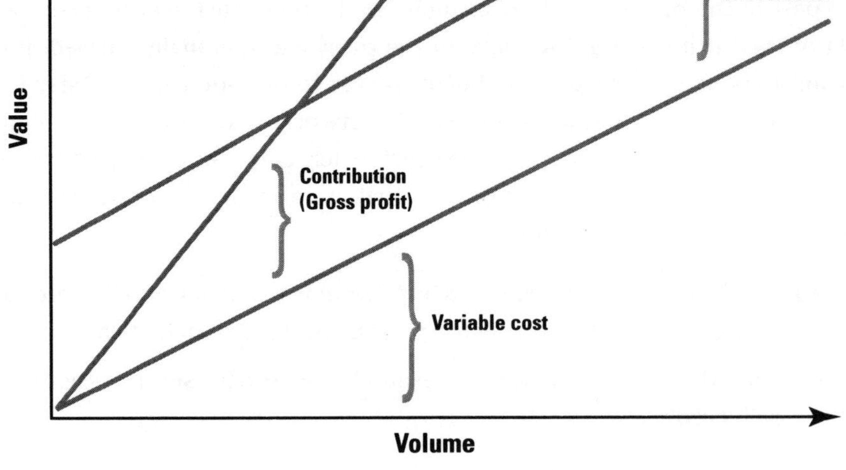

FIG 12.3: B/E FOR MARGINAL PRICING

The hope is that by the end of the financial year, all the contributions from the various jobs and products add up to more than the total overhead of the firm. This may be the case when times are good. The temptation is, however, that when times are hard, in order to be competitive, the business will price its work so as to make only small contributions above variable cost. Under these circumstances, it is frequently the case that by the end of the financial year all these contributions **do not** add up to the total overhead. Eventually the firm runs out of capital and goes bust, which is the main problem with a marginal pricing strategy.

Implications of the overhead to variable cost ratio (OH/VC)

There is one area in a service business where knowledge of variable costs versus fixed costs is vital when deciding the pricing policy of the firm.

In one case where the ratio of overhead to variable cost is high, the service marketer must adopt a pricing policy that alters the prices charged over time as the product moves towards break-even. To fail to break even in a situation like this, would be extremely dangerous for the firm, because the high overhead provides a particularly unforgiving burden.

If, however, the ratio of overhead to variable cost is low, then paradoxically there is far greater room for manoeuver, and a failure to break even is not so severely punished.

As can be seen in Figure 12.4, the angle theta (Ø) at which price P breaks even is very wide. This means that a small increment either above or below break-even has a disproportionate effect on profitability.

A good example of this is an airline. One is told that, for example, an airline route crossing the Atlantic, the cost of flying one extra passenger before or above break-even is a relatively small amount of fuel. All the other elements of cost are relatively fixed. No extra meals are delivered, no extra staff are required and there is no need for extra administration, and so forth.

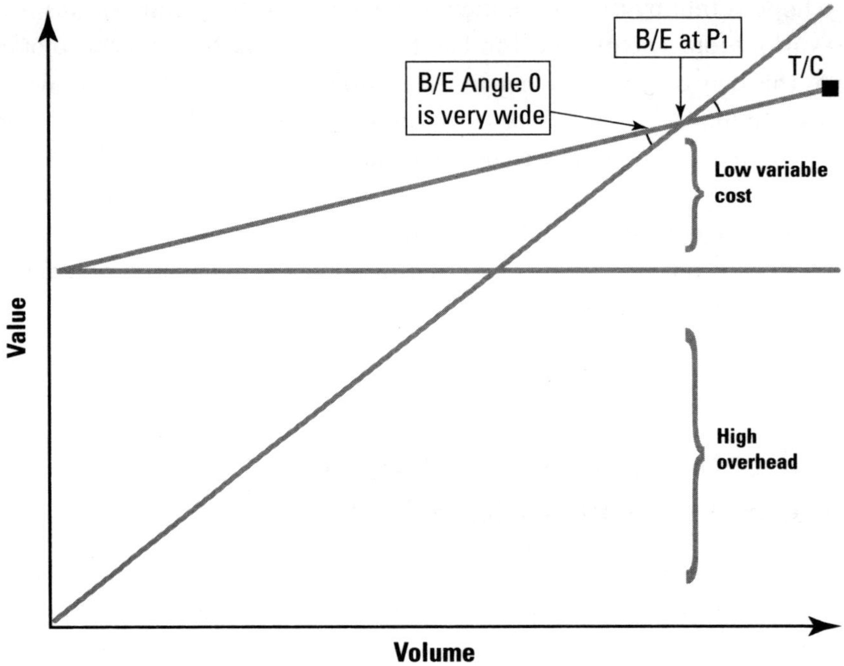

FIG 12.4: WHERE THE RATIO OF OVERHEAD TO VARIABLE COST IS HIGH

For every passenger that the plane is short of break-even, a considerable cost is incurred.

So, to take the example of a transatlantic flight:

If a given flight has (say) one Business Class passenger less than break-even, the airline will make a loss of at least £1,000 on that flight.

Alternatively, the extra revenue represented by one extra Business Class passenger over break-even, is quite considerable. Thus it would enjoy £1,000 profit if the one extra passenger does turn-up.

The losses from those flights that fall short must be made up from flights that make a profit. The strategy in such a case, therefore, must be for the organization to go for **volume**, and adopt pricing strategies which are designed specifically to achieve that end.

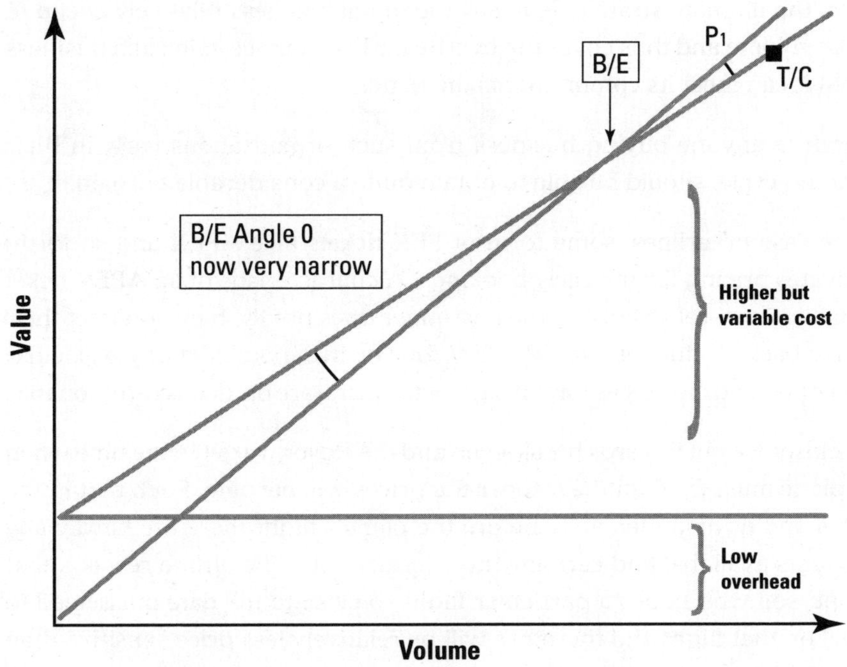

FIG 12.5: WHERE THE RATIO OF OVERHEAD TO VARIABLE COST IS LOW

However, consider Figure 12.5, here we see that where the overhead is kept particularly low as a ratio of variable cost, the amount by which a firm is going to suffer by falling short of break-even (or enjoys profit if it exceeds break-even), is relatively small. Under these circumstances the policies must be designed to go for **value**.

So for a high ratio of 'fixed' to 'variable' costs, the rule of thumb is:

- Volume dominates,

and for a low ratio,

- Value dominates.

Examples of this are found in both the airline business and the market for management training.

In exactly the same way that a product manager for an airline route is driven by volume and will have a year before the flight to try to load every seat in the plane, via PEX tickets and the like, so a management trainer will try to have about a year's worth of diary booked ahead at any one time. In both cases, the ultimate strategy is to sell the initial business relatively cheap to go for volume and thus cover the overhead. The more certain each business is that it can meet its commitments the better.

Therefore anyone buying business from such organizations early in their planning cycle, should be able to obtain quite a considerable bargain.

In the case of airlines, some form of PEX tickets (like APEX and so forth) motivates pricing for the early bookings. A characteristic of an APEX ticket is that it is non-refundable. If the passenger does not fly, they don't get their money back. So for, let's say, the first four or five months of any particular flight's booking life, prices for the back of the plane are particularly reasonable.

The closer we get towards break-even and the closer we get to the time when the plane must fly, then the steeper the prices will become. Such that in the weeks and days immediately before the plane's flight there are hardly any discounts available and certainly no special deals. The airline reasons that any person who books a particular flight so close to the date must need to travel on that flight and therefore will be relatively less price sensitive than one who has booked 12 months ahead.

At break-even the situation will change dramatically. At that point the trainer and the airline product manager know that they will cover their costs. Any extra business, particularly that booked at short notice, should therefore be charged at a premium. This is particularly true for business trainers because there is a real opportunity cost of time. At this point it will be a scarce commodity in exactly the same way as there will be relatively few seats left on the plane. So both organizations working with supply and demand on their side, can charge a premium price.

The trainer has to do this in order to ration that spare time which would otherwise be available for curriculum development and self-improvement, writing books and so forth. The airline route (product) manager will at this point give instructions to those preparing the plane for flight to maximize, if possible, the Business Class and First Class areas of the plane.

Implications of OH/VC ratios on resource capacity strategies

Although, as we have seen in early chapters, the maintenance of the quality of service delivery is most easily accomplished by maintaining sufficient resource capacity in-house, a few moments thought about this OH/VC ratio will explain why so many service organizations are tempted to become 'virtual companies'.

The cost advantages of not owning (but leasing instead) the planes, computers, booking facilities, cabin crew, flight deck crew, aircraft maintenance facilities and so forth are extraordinarily tempting.

Ownership of all this resource will incur a phenomenally large overhead. Whereas if the service firm could farm out the business to a sub-contractor or two, as and when required, these costs become a variable cost and the pressures on price to go for volume rather than value evaporate. In the case of an airline, this can represent a tremendous extra profitability per seat.

In addition, airlines and any other similar service businesses would have much lower break-even points with less sleepless nights for the financial director.

Exercise

'Applied pricing strategies'

What pricing strategy is the most appropriate for each of the following?:

- Classic French restaurant
- Pay per view TV exclusive sports event
- A service setting-up and managing websites for small businesses
- New package holiday on the Albanian coast
- A range of training packages offered by an independent management trainer
- A 'gold' charge or credit card
- Room hire in a Travel Lodge specializing in rooms for business travelers.

References

72 *For a comprehensive introduction to pricing please see 'Mastering Marketing' (by this author) Chapter 4, Part 2.*

THIRTEEN

Seriously seeking the feedback

THIRTEEN

Seriously seeking the feedback

Introduction

"Marketing is a dialogue over time with a specific group of customers..."

Professor M. MacDonald

"Know your opponent and your battlefield as well as you know yourself... and you can fight a hundred battles without disaster..."

After Sun Tzu

Successful service businesses critically depend on building relationships, therefore the listening part of the communication process is absolutely vital. As Tom Peters says:

- *"Listening **IS** part of the product". We call this 'listening activity' a Market Intelligence System, which consists of:*
- *A 'Market Information System' (MIS), i.e. What is going on in the marketplace? – and*
- *A 'Customer Information System' (CIS), i.e. What is happening to our customer turnover, needs, preferences, perceptions, expectations, levels of delight or otherwise?*

Additionally it is important to realize that market (or marketing) research is only one part of the overall MIS/CIS via which the business manager listens to the customers and their influencers. The totality of this information we call the Marketing Intelligence System. In this chapter we are going to concentrate on just this part of the total management system of the business.

Categories of information

But before we examine the various tools, it would be useful to define the different categories of information.

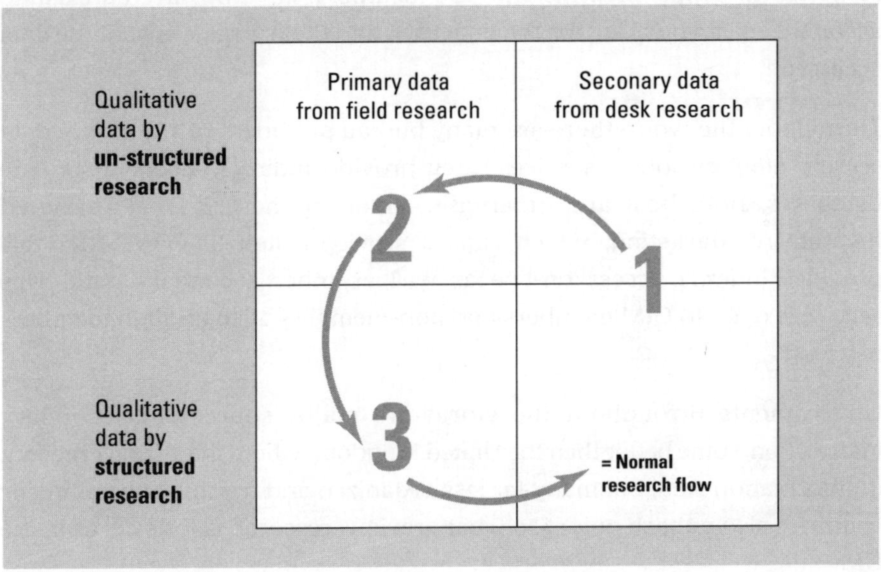

FIG 13.1: TYPES OF INFORMATION AVAILABLE FOR MIS/CIS

Essentially there are four categories of information. They fall into a two by two matrix as above – in order of the research process, they are:

- **Secondary data** – second-hand data that some other organization has gathered at some other time, for some other purpose but yours.
- **Primary data** – information gathered direct from the market, either via a research agency, or by your organization.
- **Qualitative data** – unstructured data, often for initial exploratory purposes because we don't know what the issues are with our customers. We may think we know, but we are not our own typical customers.
- **Quantitative data** – the information has numbers and proportions associated with them and with the right size and type of sample will also have confidence levels and statistical significance to the point that we can make management decisions based on this information, with confidence.

Secondary data via 'desk research'

The major benefit of secondary data is that it can be accessed at a very modest cost compared to the cost of primary research, another is the speed with which the data can be obtained. However, direct access to a 'host' database is usually restricted to people or firms who are members, i.e. they have an existing account and can be billed for the time used and the per page cost of the data accessed.

Throughout the world there are many bureau providers of secondary data search, amongst other services, they provide indirect access to on-line databases, both host and otherwise. Amongst these is The Chartered Institute of Marketing, which runs a service called 'INFOMARK', this provides indirect access on-line as well as other secondary data. This service is open to CIM members and non-members alike (though members pay less).

Governments throughout the world are major sources of secondary information, some better than the United Kingdom (where there is no Freedom of Information Act), but many far less organized and fruitful. Several major countries also publish guides to what previous research is for sale, as in the UK.

Secondary data will be used to bring the business manager up to speed with the main issues in the market, and to identify those areas where information gaps exist. These gaps, if material to the objectives of the research, will now need to be filled via primary research.

However, it is dangerous to accept any secondary data at its face value. The researcher should never forget that it is 'second-hand', i.e. obtained by someone else, at some other time, for some other purpose than the researcher's objectives. It should therefore always be tested for **impartiality**, **validity**, **currency**, and **reliability**. In this context these are taken as meaning:

Impartiality

'Partial data' is produced when there is a 'hidden agenda' to the research. Often research is carried out to 'prove a point', or the data has been edited with such a motive. Trade associations, and industry groups are notorious for slanting the data they present to the outside world. The 'sharp' manager must ensure that he/she is satisfied that whatever bias exists, (some bias will always be present) it does not put his/her research objectives in jeopardy.

Validity

That is to say that the research measures what it purports to measure. A notable example to illustrate are the 'Hawthorn Studies' where the initial research was to measure assembly shop productivity as a function of working conditions. The hypothesis being that, 'The better the conditions, the higher the workforce productivity'. A specific variable under investigation was lighting as an aspect of the working conditions. Better lighting did seem to result in higher productivity, but when the quality of lighting was reduced, productivity did not decline apace. Later research was able to show that assembly shop workers were responding to heightened levels of management attention, they had never seen managers on the shop floor before, let alone so many.

Currency

How up-to-date is the information? The more current, then the more relevant and useful the data is. The older the data the less reliable it will probably be.

Reliability

This topic asks whether the research methodology is up to the job? A simple test is: would the marketer be satisfied with the way this research were carried out if he/she were to commission it, and to pay out of their own budget?

The author does not expect a large majority of readers to be familiar with marketing research methodology (or indeed any other research methodology), so if not, then the author advises the business manager to seek the opinion of those who are familiar with research methodology, preferably for marketing, and who don't charge a fortune. This type of person can most frequently be found in business schools and universities. They would be flattered to be asked for their opinion, and normally they charge far less than market research consultants.

Primary information via field research

Primary research is conducted to fill information gaps that the secondary data has not been able to satisfy.

Primary data can be obtained via a matrix of research approaches.

AD HOC vs. MULTI-CLIENT on the one axis

and

QUALITATIVE vs. QUANTITATIVE on the other.

Ad hoc studies

The research is normally commissioned direct by the business managers responsible. It is usually conducted on his/her behalf, this is most frequently known as 'ad hoc' (some refer to it as 'tailor made').

The benefits are that:

- the data obtained is the copyright of the client commissioning the research,
- the fact of the research being conducted and for whom can be confidential,
- the client has full control of the process,
- the research focuses entirely on what the client requires, and
- the timing of the research will be to suit the client.

The trade-offs are:

- the research will be more expensive, and
- in many cases it will take much longer.

Multi-client studies

These fall into three distinct categories:

i) Syndicated studies instigated by a group of firms in an industry. This study is then farmed out to be conducted by a research agency,

ii) Industry studies originated by the research agency, and

iii) Omnibus studies – where the client buys one or more questions on a study that will be conducted as a regular event.

In the latter two types of study, it is not clear who has ownership of the copyright to the data obtained, though it is general opinion that the agency conducting owns the copyright in item (ii); and the individual clients only own the copyright to the results from their questions in item (iii).

The main benefits of a multi-client approach are primarily cost. The costs of this type of research are shared by a group of firms; to the extent that, particularly for (i) and (ii), firms would otherwise not be able to afford, and therefore may not do, the research.

Qualitative research

Perhaps the largest source of error in any data collection of primary data is the assumption that 'we know what is important to the customer' when in fact 'we' often do not. Issues that are important to the customer are referred to as being 'salient' and when we combine this with the degree of importance – i.e. how much are they important to the customer, it is referred to as saliency.

The only reliable way to obtain insights into this area of customer motivation is to create the circumstances whereby they can tell us about what motivates them without the researcher prompting them in any way.

This so-called 'unstructured research' is often exploratory by nature. There are many ways of conducting qualitative research, ranging from in-depth interviews to focus group discussions.

Qualitative data is obtained using so called 'unstructured research' techniques. There will usually not be a questionnaire, rather a so-called 'topics list'. Questions are nearly all in 'open' format, employing the classic 'six honest serving men' of Kipling fame, (i.e. what, why, when, where, how, and who).

These research methods all require a high level of interviewing skills during the data capture, and interpretive skills during data analysis.

The implications are that the business manager should treat the findings of such research with caution.

There is insufficient space to allow us to go into the details of the 'focus group' format or techniques. That information will be available on request should you visit the author's website.

However a golden rule for qualitative research

(For the guidance of the wise and the adherence of fools) Never, (well, hardly ever) make important marketing decisions, particularly those where a substantial amount of money may be a stake, on the basis of qualitative research alone.

Quantitative research

The methodologies employed in quantitative research techniques are frequently referred to as 'structured'. The quantitative data is captured via the use of an 'instrument' such as a questionnaire, diary or audit most of which can either be self administered, (such as by postal or e-mail questionnaire) or response can be obtained via a personal interview conducted face to face or by telephone.

The quantitative data is captured from a controlled sample of respondents. This sample may be designed either to represent the target group, or to ensure that all elements of the target group are adequately represented in the data obtained.

Market/customer information systems

Market/ing research is only one aspect of the totality of information sources that a marketer should employ to keep informed about his/her market.

A compound of a Market Information System [MIS], and a Customer Information System [CIS] can provide the business manager with the basis to make a good 80% of his/her marketing decisions.

Let's start by comparing and contrasting the two:

The relationship between market/ing research and a MIS/CIS

MARKET/ING RESEARCH	MARKET/CUSTOMER
SYSTEM/S	INFORMATION
Short duration High intensity	Continuous Low level
(Relatively) expensive activity when contracted out – in-house. • The 'snapshot' • The 'surgeon's Knife' • Invasive surgery • It can aggravate the marketplace	Inexpensive activity – Often conducted • The 'movie' • Preventative medicine
THE SORT OF ISSUES ADDRESSED • Size of market, • How comprised by prospect and by competitor	• Customer satisfaction • Trends in the market • Buying behavior and • Motives, price sensitivity etc

Marketing research is a snapshot in time. It is of short duration, highly expensive and a very intensive activity which has the undesirable side effect, if used too frequently, of annoying the very people with whom the marketer is trying to build a relationship (i.e. the customer), particularly in business to business [B2B] markets.

The need to resort to market/ing research can often be caused by the non-existence of, or the poor operation of, either a CIS or MIS or both.

Marketing research does have its uses, in fact there are some marketing situations where it is the only viable tool and it should be reserved for those situations (such as new product development, surveys of staff attitude, surveys of the competitors customers and their attitudes towards not only the competitor but one's own firm). The use of marketing research outside these areas of activity can be seen as an admission of the failure of the basic Market or Customer Information System that the marketer should have in place.

The MIS or CIS

These should be designed so as to be capable of providing enough information to make 80% of the marketing decisions that need to be addressed without recourse to external market research. Indeed a good market/customer information system is the 'preventive medicine' that means that the marketer will rarely have any recourse to the 'surgery' of market research, (outside of the areas instanced above).

The principle is that the marketer uses the MIS/CIS to gather information on a continuous basis. In addition to its information providing role, by being seen to measure, the MIS/CIS becomes part of the marketing management set of tools. The measurement aspects of the tool is sweetened (part of human nature is to resist being measured) via the use of rewards for the staff concerned, that are built within the system. This is a whole topic in its own right and will not be covered here.

The design of the MIS/CIS starts with the decision as to what should be measured and how frequently. This in turn emanates from a clear understanding of what the business manager wants to do. The system should be designed to produce information that will assist in the improvement of the 'product' from the customer's point of view. Therefore, the business manager must establish and maintain an understanding of what issues are salient to the customer's perception of quality.

For example, for a conference center, research conducted into what matters in coffee breaks shows that a priority concern of the attendees is not how hot the coffee is, (the management's opinion), but how fast the coffee is served. Nor is the availability of biscuits as important as the proximity of toilets and telephones.

A good MIS/CIS incorporates a continuous review of secondary data. A most valuable part of which will be a cuttings book circulated on a need to know basis to everyone in the business team.

The good business manager will keep themselves up to date with the issues and criteria that are salient to customers via a program of regular qualitative research with focus groups comprised of customers.

In other circumstances, particularly with products which are positioned towards the intellectual property end of the spectrum, such as 'consultancy', this information gathering is more often conducted via semi-in-depth unstructured interviews on a one-to-one basis.

The MIS/CIS tools

The main management tool consists of two aspects of quantitative data gathering ('what you can't measure you can't manage'), one is active, the other passive.

The passive aspect relies on the customer taking the initiative. It consisting of such facilities as freephone numbers, plus some form of incentive to encourage their propensity to buy at some time in the future.

CUSTOMER COMPLAINT ANALYSIS

The aim is to encourage customer complaints via the use of freephone numbers and some form of incentive to make contact. This active side consists of such practices as (so called) mystery shopping (see below), as well as customer surveys, and internal staff attitude surveys. If service is used to add value to the product, the management of moments of truth, (i.e. when one's own people are delivering the service), particularly requires that the morale, attitudes and opinions of the people delivering the service be kept under surveillance.

MYSTERY SHOPPING

This is a double-sided coin. One side consists of monitoring the competition. We can always learn things from the competition even if it's only from their mistakes. (As they are still in existence so they must be doing something right.)

The second side of the mystery shopping coin is the constant surveillance of how well the marketer's own firm delivers service.

This requires that there be some well defined 'action standards' to provide yardsticks against which the delivery of the service can be monitored.

Some of the things to be continually measured when the contact is by telephone are, for example:

- The speed with which telephones are answered,
- The form of words that are used when answering the telephone,
- How customers are transferred to other departments,
- Product knowledge, (how comprehensive and up-to-date is it) etc.
- Some organizations term these 'service points' and they would include such things when face to face as: making eye contact, making physical contact and using the customer's name. (These are all so called 'positive strokes', the absence of them are 'negative strokes'.)
- The marketer, when designing mystery shopping for internal surveillance, should ensure that it is not used as a means to discipline people, but seen as a tool to identify areas that require training to improve.

Customer surveys

If these are held on a frequent basis, they can be expensive. The main source of cost will derive from the difficulty of obtaining a consistent sample, be that a representative sample, or one where each of the sub groups of customers are adequately represented (there is a difference).

This cost can be greatly ameliorated via the use of customer banks, or customer panels:

A panel

This is a standing sample of business customers, very similar to a user group. The panel is so designed as to be representative of the market. Each and every member of the panel (respondent) will be surveyed every time data is captured. This requires skilful management to make sure that people on the panel do not turn into professional respondents (that is to say behave abnormally and therefore cease to be representative).

A customer bank

This is a reservoir of customers who may only be interviewed once during their time within the bank.

Respondents for such banks are recruited from regular surveys of the general customer and prospect universe.

Recruitment will occur via the use of a 'recruitment question', usually at the end of the initial survey questionnaire. This recruiting question will indicate to the respondent that the firm would like to stay in touch for the purposes of gathering information in the future. It will additionally point out that there will always be an incentive in return for a response and will ask the customer's permission to put their name and address on a database for this purpose.

If the respondent is favorably inclined, they are then asked for the most convenient days of the week, time of the day and so forth when they may be contacted.

Filters should be in place to ensure that no respondent is included in the database more than once (at any one time). Subsequently data can be captured from the bank via a 'dipstick approach', (i.e. a low cost, fast turn round research using telephone or e-mail questioning), using very small but highly defined samples. Participating respondents can be tracked over time via the use of several dipsticks or alternatively by the provision of diaries.

There are some important issues to address when surveying staff and/or business customers, either directly, or via panels or banks. The most important is **how** data is captured.

Postal or self-completed questionnaires frequently have very low response rates. These response rates can be improved if the panel or the bank is well managed.

A **Telephone** survey will enjoy a higher contact level, but over time, particularly for a panel, it can seem intrusive and therefore suffer reduced response rates in the long-term.

It is often worth considering employing a combination of the two, a short telephone call alerting the respondent to a self-completing questionnaire, which is on its way. This approach will usually allow for longer questionnaires leading to increased data richness.

Again, if service is used to add value, the marketer must make sure that the data captured enables the effective management of Service Delivery.

To do this it must meet the information needs of the key customers for the product or service. As mentioned above, it must expressly measure the customer's overall satisfaction on salient issues, i.e. those things that are important to customers.

At this point it is worth noting that some issues which are salient to some customers, may not be salient to others. An indication of satisfaction with an issue that is salient should be considered therefore, as more important than an indication of satisfaction against one that is not. Not to address this phenomenon will be like comparing apples with pears.

When designing the 'instrument' it is important not to include inappropriate questions (i.e. ones that customers have no basis on which to answer truthfully).

The MIS/CIS strategy should measure customer satisfaction and internal staff attitudes on a regular basis and with a frequency to allow time between each of the surveys for action to be taken and to have an effect before the next measurement is conducted. However, it must also be recent enough for the data to be pertinent to the issues of the day.

The good marketer must be absolutely clear about the difference between the measurement of a symptom, and diagnosing the cause. '**Symptom**', e.g. such as increasing customer dissatisfaction; '**Cause**', e.g. which can be anything from 'out of stock situations' through to longer queues to, staff rudeness etc.

Senior managers in a service business must constantly test the results of everything that has been 'found' with that question, "Are we looking at a cause, or a symptom?"

Causes we can address, symptoms need more digging!

Exercise

1. For your service business, decide your information objectives for a particular MIS/CIS you wish to put in place. Then draw-up a feed-back mechanism to deliver this information along the guidelines discussed in this chapter.
2. Say how you would manage this process.

INDEX

L

M

N

O

Q

R

S

T

U

V